GREENHOUSE GARDENING

Beginner's Guide to Growing Your Own Vegetables, Fruits and Herbs All Year-Round and Learn How to Quickly Build Your Own Greenhouse Garden

**by
Rachel Martin**

© Copyright 2019 by Rachel Martin - All rights reserved.

This book is provided with the sole purpose of giving relevant information on a specific topic for which every reasonable effort has been made to ensure that it is both accurate and reasonable. Nevertheless, by purchasing this book, you consent to the fact that the author and the publisher are in no way experts on the topics contained herein, regardless of any claims as such that may be made within. As such, any suggestions or recommendations that are made within are done so purely for entertainment value. It is recommended that you always consult a professional prior to undertaking any of the advice or techniques discussed within.

This is a legally binding declaration that is considered valid and fair by both the Committee of Publishers Association and the American Bar Association and should be considered as legally binding within the United States.

The reproduction, transmission, and duplication of any of the content found herein, including any specific or extended information, will be done as an illegal act regardless of the end form that the information ultimately takes. This includes copied versions of the work—whether physical, digital, or audio—unless express consent of the Publisher is provided beforehand. Any additional rights reserved.

Furthermore, the information that can be found within the pages described forthwith shall be considered both accurate and truthful when it comes to the recounting of facts. As such, any use, correct or incorrect, of the provided information will render the Publisher free of responsibility as to the actions taken outside of their direct purview. Regardless, there are zero scenarios where the original author or the Publisher can be deemed liable in any fashion for any damages or hardships that may result from any of the information discussed herein.

Additionally, the information in the following pages is intended only for informational purposes and should thus be thought of as universal. As befitting its nature, it is presented without assurance regarding its prolonged validity or interim quality. Trademarks that are mentioned are done without written consent and can in no way be considered an endorsement from the trademark holder.

TABLE OF CONTENTS

Introduction 1

PART ONE *Building Your Own Greenhouse* 3

Chapter One *Why Should I Build A Greenhouse?* 3

Chapter Two *Types Of Greenhouses* 8

Chapter Three *Planning Your Greenhouse* 14

Chapter Four *Greenhouse Essentials* 21

Chapter Five *Maximizing Your Greenhouse Space* 27

Chapter Six *Seasonal Preparation and Care* 31

Part Two *Growing in Your Greenhouse* 35

Chapter Seven *What to Plant in Your Greenhouse* 35

Chapter Eight *Starting Seeds* 44

Chapter Nine *Caring for Your Plants* 50

Chapter Ten *Year-Round Growing* 60

Chapter Eleven *Common Greenhouse Problems* 67

Conclusion 75

Description 77

INTRODUCTION

Are you looking for a new way to garden? Do you want to create your own space where you can grow plants and collect produce year round? If so, you have come to the right place!

In this book, we are going to learn all about greenhouse gardening. As you probably know, greenhouses are special outdoor buildings made specifically for growing plants. They allow you to create the perfect environment for growth in any season. They are good for any climate but are especially helpful in areas where the weather takes away the possibility of year-round, outdoor gardening. They can be used to grow any type of plant—from vegetables and herbs to tropical plant variations.

We will start by explaining the benefits of greenhouses. We will learn about the different types of greenhouses and what they are best used for. We will then look into how you can build yourself your very own greenhouse. We will talk about DIY options, greenhouse construction kits, and more. We will go through a planning checklist that will help you to decide exactly how you want your greenhouse to be designed. This checklist will touch on things like location, size, flooring, framing, and much more.

After we cover everything there is to know about greenhouses, we will look into how you can garden inside them. We will start by discussing what you can plant in a greenhouse. In this chapter, we will provide you with a wide variety of ideas to help you figure out what you would most enjoy growing in your new year-round plant home.

We will then move into the topic of planting seeds. We will go through the best places to buy your seeds, the best soil to use, and the best containers to plant them in. After covering seeds, we will talk through how to care for the plants in your greenhouse after they sprout from the ground. This chapter will contain a large amount of useful and necessary information—from lighting and temperature to pollination of plants in a place without bees. We will talk about how to time your plants so that they are able to provide a year-round supply of crops.

After we have covered everything that you need to know in order to create your greenhouse and grow healthy plants inside of it, we will go through a list of common problems that can happen in a greenhouse. We will look into how you can solve these problems, as well as ways to prevent them from happening in the first place.

When you finish reading this book, you will be a greenhouse expert—even if you have never stepped foot inside of one of these buildings before. You will know why greenhouses are talked about so often, as well as all of the benefits that can come from growing your plants inside of them. You'll be able to build a greenhouse from the ground up and create a harvest from simple seeds. You will know how to solve any problems that may arise so that your plants always remain healthy and strong. If you are ready to open your mind and discover a new way to enjoy gardening, turn the page and begin your greenhouse gardening journey now!

PART ONE
BUILDING YOUR OWN GREENHOUSE

CHAPTER ONE
Why Should I Build A Greenhouse?

Before we dive too deep into building your own greenhouse and doing all of your plantings inside of it, let's look at why greenhouses are so great. In this chapter, we will look into the top ten advantages to greenhouse gardening. We are sure that by the time that you reach the end of these ten reasons, you will be daydreaming about the moment you get to start on your own greenhouse adventure.

1. The main and most obvious benefit of greenhouses is that they give you a longer growing season. Depending on how you design and construct your greenhouse and depending on what type of climate you live in, this extension could add a couple of months onto your typical summer-growing season, or it could extend your time to the point that you could garden all year long. Greenhouses extend your growing season because they provide the perfect growing atmosphere inside of them. This makes you as the greenhouse owner and designer in charge of how long your gardening season lasts—when typically, that would be left up to the weather.

2. If we're playing off of this first reason, greenhouses also give you the ability to keep your plants safe during inclement weather. Normally, if there were a thunderstorm and flash flooding, you would have to sit inside just hoping that your plants would survive the night. If there were strong winds coming through, you would have to worry that they would break the stems of your plants and prevent them from being able to produce a crop for the season. With a greenhouse,

your entire garden is protected by a roof and sturdy walls. No weather will be able to affect your plants when you keep them safe.

3. While speaking of keeping your plants safe, greenhouses also help to protect your garden from critters that live in the wild. Most people who grow gardens have sad stories about rabbits eating their tomatoes before they could get to them to harvest or birds flying down to steal their strawberries before they are ripe enough for humans to eat. With a greenhouse, no animals or critters are able to get inside. This means that your produce will be safe up until the moment that you are able to harvest from your plants.

4. Outdoor gardens are not only affected by furry critters like rabbits and birds. They also are often discovered by bugs. Some types of insects, like bees and ants, should be welcomed in the outdoor garden since bees help to pollinate plants and ants help to turn the soil, allowing extra nutrients to reach the roots of the plants. Other bugs, however, can be pests to a garden. Some bugs may eat your crop or even cause your plants to become diseased and die. Because a greenhouse is a closed-off space, it helps to keep your garden safe from these unwanted bugs as well.

5. With those pest-like bugs in mind, we will move into our next greenhouse advantage. When you grow a greenhouse, you do not have to worry about unwanted bugs in your garden. Because of this, you have no need for pesticides and other dangerous bug-related chemicals in your garden. This helps you to avoid the use of chemicals in your garden and helps to keep your produce safer.

6. Without pesticides, you are one step closer to growing an organic garden. If you are interested in going organic and growing a garden that is completely chemical free, a greenhouse makes this a much easier task to handle. Typically, in a greenhouse, you will be doing some sort of variety of container gardening. Because of this, you can choose high-quality soils and growing media that eliminate your need for chemical fertilizers. With no need for

pesticides or chemical fertilizers, having an organic garden inside a greenhouse is easy to do.

7. A greenhouse also allows you to grow any type of plant that you would like to grow. Normally if you live in a climate where you can only garden during a few specific months out of the year, you would have a hard time growing something like tropical plants. You would have to keep them inside your home most of the time, and if you wanted to have an entire tropical garden, this would not work out well. With a greenhouse, you have a dedicated space for your plants that do not have to follow along with the climate you live in, so you can grow anything.

8. Greenhouses really live up to having "green" in their name. With a greenhouse, you have the ability to be more environmentally friendly than you can be with a regular, outdoor garden. This is not only because the design of the greenhouse reduces the need for heat and extra lights, but you have more control over your space, so you are able to be more conservative with water as well. It also gives you a chance to add a larger amount of plants to the Earth, which is a great environmentally friendly effort as well as the things that we have already mentioned.

9. Because greenhouses are able to have their environments perfected and they do not have to rely on unreliable factors like the sun or air temperature in order to survive, plants in greenhouses are able to thrive. This means that if you are growing fruits, vegetables, or herbs, your plants will be able to provide you with healthier food than they would be able to if your garden was outside.

10. Scientists have found that if you are surrounded by living things like plants, your rate of depression and anxiety drops dramatically. Being surrounded by greenery is great for stress relief and helping with mental illnesses. It is such a powerful force that many therapists include greenery in their offices and some psychologists even hold group therapy courses inside of greenhouses. With a greenhouse, you can feel these stress relieving feelings whenever you

need to. This is a great tool for fighting any type of stress or mental illness, especially seasonal depression since you have a warm, living green place to go to all year round.

Overall, it is clear that greenhouses have many benefits. Just in case it is not clear yet, let's look into why you should grow a greenhouse and how these benefits can affect your life. We believe that every single person on Earth would benefit from growing plants in a greenhouse, but it would especially help you if you happen to find yourself in any of the following situations or scenarios.

If you love to grow plants but do not have space, build a greenhouse. It will provide you with all of the space you need to be dedicated solely to your plants. If you love to garden but find yourself only able to grow plants a few months out of the year, build a greenhouse. It will give you the ability to extend your growing season as long as you want to, even if you want your garden to keep growing on a year-round basis. If you have sad experiences of losing garden crops to summer storms, build a greenhouse. You will never have to experience this loss of your hard work ever again. If you are looking to grow an organic garden, but you seem to struggle with insect infestations or poor soil, build a greenhouse. These factors will be able to be controlled with ease with no need to bring chemicals into the mix—if you are looking for a cheap way to feed your family, build a greenhouse. It will allow you to grow enough food to provide for a large amount of what your family consumes. The cost of the greenhouse will soon be outweighed by all of the money that you save from not having to buy as many groceries. The fewer trips to the grocery store are a great positive note as well. If you are looking to be more environmentally friendly, build a greenhouse. It will allow you to put more plants on the Earth as well as to conserve energy and water in your gardening practice. If you want to grow a type of plant that your specific climate does not support well, build a greenhouse. You will be able to grow anything inside of it that you would like to grow. If you struggle with stress or mental illness, build a greenhouse. Being surrounded by living greenery that you work hard to support will be a great tool in helping you cope and thrive in life.

Overall, we believe that building a greenhouse and growing a garden inside of it truly could benefit the life of any person. Throughout the rest of the book, we will look into the details of how to do this, and these benefits will continue to be weaved throughout the pages. If you are not convinced that growing a greenhouse is right for you yet, we are sure that you will be by the time you reach the last page of this book.

CHAPTER TWO
Types Of Greenhouses

In this chapter, we are going to look into the different types of greenhouses. It is important to know about the different types of greenhouses and what they are best used for so that you are able to choose the best type of greenhouse for you. We are going to start by looking into the different structures that greenhouses can be made in. We will then look at some specific details that you may want to consider when deciding how exactly to build your greenhouse for the biggest personalized benefit. Lastly, we will look into different building techniques that you can use to build the greenhouse of your dreams.

In order to start creating that greenhouse dream, let's look at the big picture. There are seven different structures that greenhouses are usually made in. They include post and rafter, a-frame, gothic arch, hoop house, lean-to, window, and cold frame. We will explain each of these greenhouse types in detail below.

A post and rafter greenhouse takes the structure that you may consider as a typical house structure. It has a pointed roof like you would imagine seeing in a child's drawing of a house. This is a very common structure for greenhouse building. It is typically made with wooden posts and has strong support in its roof with rafters as well, which is where it gets its name of course. One of the best things about it is that it is very strong. If you live in an area with strong winds that happen fairly often, this greenhouse structure may be a good choice for you. It is also a good structure space if you have a large, open area to build it in since it does take up more space than other types of structures. Because it takes up more space though, it also provides you with more space for planting.

Next, let's look into a-frame greenhouses. These are simple to build because they have fewer materials than other types of greenhouses. It is a triangular structure, so its two side walls lean together to make a point at its top. This makes its walls and roof basically the same pieces. This can make it harder to fit as many plants inside since the walls are so slanted, but you can overcome this obstacle pretty easily with some creative shelving ideas. It is nice because it is easy to put together. It is still a good structure for if you have a large open space for it to go in, similar to the post and rafter models. The main difference between these two models is that an A-frame greenhouse is lighter and easier to build.

A gothic arch greenhouse is a common option as well. The frame of this greenhouse is built in a semicircle shape. This frame can easily be covered with plastic sheeting, which helps the building process to be pretty simple. It again requires a large open space for it to be built in. The rounded shape makes this type of greenhouse a particularly good choice for people who live in snowy or rainy climates because the snow and rain have nowhere to get caught on the rounded surfaces.

The hoop house structure for greenhouses is pretty similar to the gothic arch structure. It is again easy to build, and it is again good for areas that have a lot of rain or a lot of snow. The qualities that are unique to the hoop house are that it is the cheapest structure of greenhouse to build, so it is a good choice if you find yourself to be on a tight budget, and it is a little bit easier to squeeze into small yard spaces if you do not have enough room to build one of the previous structures. It is, however, less sturdy than the options that we have looked into before it.

Next, let's look into a structure called a lean-to greenhouse. A lean-to greenhouse can be built to be leaning up to another structure on your property. This allows for one of the walls of the greenhouse to simply be the wall of the structure that it is built up against. This is both an affordable way to build a greenhouse as well as a great option for small spaces. It is even better protected from strong winds since it is built up against such a stable base. One thing that is not so great about this structure of greenhouse is that it is harder to heat. This is because some of the heat may be lost on the wall of the home. It also has to be built on the south side of a home because that is the place where it will get the best sunlight.

Our next two greenhouse options are for people who do not have space in their yards to build a new greenhouse structure. They are much smaller and do not provide all of the same great benefits as larger, walk-in greenhouses do, but they are still better than not being able to grow in a greenhouse at all.

The first small greenhouse option is window greenhouses. This works best if you have greenhouse windows, or bay windows, that stick out from the walls of your house. If you have these types of windows, they are great for plants because the sun can hit the plants from more than just one angle. These windows do a pretty good job at providing a greenhouse effect for your indoor plants. If you do not have these types of windows, you can use something called a window farm. Window farms can be used in almost any window. It is basically a hydroponic system that grows plants in water in a structure that is made to sit in your window sill. These are small, and you cannot have a large garden in them, but they still provide the greenhouse effect for people who do not have big yards or even bay windows to grow their plants in.

The second small greenhouse option we will look into is something that still sits outside like a normal greenhouse instead of sitting in your home's windows. These greenhouses are called cold frames. Cold frames are greenhouse boxes that you can plant in. They provide the same effects that a larger, walk-in greenhouse would provide but instead of being able to walk inside of them to garden, you lift up the top and garden from them like a typical garden box. They are a cheap option for outdoor gardening that can still greatly extend the growing season that your area's natural climate provides you with.

Now that we have looked into the different types of greenhouses, it is time for you to decide which structure is right for you. If you have no backyard but have beautiful bay windows inside of your home, you may want to consider a window greenhouse. If you have a large outdoor space with an open field on the south side of your home, you may want to consider a Post-and-Rafter greenhouse. To decide what type of greenhouse you would like to build, start by looking at your space. What do you have room for? Where could your greenhouse go? Then, consider what you want from your greenhouse. Do you want to grow enough food to feed your family? Do you just want to try out some new herb growing techniques? Lastly, consider your skill level. What can you manage to build by yourself or with the help of your friends and family? After taking these factors into consideration, go back and look into the details of each of the greenhouses we talked about. Which one best suits your needs?

Picking the type of structure is not the last step in deciding what type of greenhouse to build, however. Next, you need to decide which route you would like to take in order to build the greenhouse of your dreams. You could go the completely DIY route, you could get a greenhouse building kit, or you could get a used greenhouse and turn it into exactly what you want it to be.

First, let's look at what to consider before deciding to go the completely DIY route when building your greenhouse. If you choose this option, you need to be prepared to do a lot of work. Building a greenhouse from scratch will require a lot of knowledge as well. It will help if you or someone you know has a background in construction. If you know how to go to Home Depot and get the type of wood you need, and if you know how to measure and cut wood, you will be off to a good start. You will need tools for this route as well. If you do not own the correct tools you could borrow them from a friend or see if your city has a tool library that they could be borrowed from; just make sure that you know how to use the tools that you need in a safe manner.

If building a greenhouse from scratch seems like it might be a little bit too difficult, but you still want to do some of the work in putting things together and using tools, you could consider buying a greenhouse kit. These kits come with everything you need to build the greenhouse structure from the boards to the nails and screws. To build these, you just need to know how to read an instruction guide, and you need to have access to tools. Again, you could reach out to a friend or family member or a nearby tool library for this necessity. Greenhouse kits are going to be a little bit more expensive than if you chose to build your greenhouse completely on your own, but if this is a building level that you are more comfortable with then the added price may be worth the extra benefits.

Lastly, let's look into what to do if you are really not comfortable building a greenhouse from scratch or from a kit with just the pieces and an instruction guide, but you still really want to make your own customized growing space. In this scenario, you could buy a used greenhouse and simply turn it into exactly what you want. In this case, the structure is already put together for you but you are still able to do a little work, and you are able to make you very own greenhouse space. This option may cost more than the previous two options, but if you are unable to put a structure together on your own, then this may be the best way to go about building your own greenhouse.

When you are considering what type of greenhouse to build and exactly how to do it, you need to look at the structure shape and the way that you are going to make it, but there are some other factors to consider as well. First, you will want to decide if you want to build your greenhouse out of wood or out of aluminum. Aluminum can be easier to put together, but wood posts are typically sturdier and will last longer, especially if you live in areas that can have strong winds fairly often.

You will also need to decide if you want glass or polycarbonate panes. In the past, glass was the most popular option. Recently, however, more people have been choosing to build with polycarbonate panels. These panes hold up better, and they are able to insulate your greenhouse better than glass. Glass lets in more light, but the light that polycarbonate panes let in is diffused, so it is actually a better light when looking into the growth of plants. The only advantages that glass possesses are that it lasts longer if it is not broken and that it does not need any specialized treatments, while polycarbonate panels do. When looking into this decision, decide if you will be able to handle the upkeep that comes with polycarbonate panels. If you can, they are the best choice with your plant's health and ability to thrive in mind.

Another option is to consider if you would like to build your structure as a half-brick greenhouse. These greenhouses are built with brick on the bottom where light does not really need to come in, and glass or polycarbonate panes on the rest of the structure. This allows for a sturdier base. It helps the greenhouse to last longer and also provides a nice aesthetic look to the structure.

With all of these options in mind, you should be able to pick out the type of greenhouse that is best for you. You can choose the size and shape that will work best for your area as well as the building plan that you are the most comfortable with. You can decide between aluminum and wood as well as between glass and polycarbonate. You can consider half-brick or typical greenhouse structures. With all of these choices made, you will be able to imagine the greenhouse that is absolutely perfect for your space and for your needs as a gardener.

CHAPTER THREE
Planning Your Greenhouse

Now that we have looked into how to plan the outside of your structure, we need to learn about how to plan the inside of your structure. This is the space that your plants will grow in and the space that you will see whenever you are out taking care of them. It needs to be beautiful and functional. In this chapter, we are going to look into some things that your greenhouse needs to be capable of, as well as what you need to plan in order to make these things work. We will look into location, size, air flow, humidity, light, heating, cooling, flooring, and glazing. We will also look into a few additional things you need to keep in mind when planning your greenhouse like safety and when to secure it from the wind.

First, when starting the process of planning your greenhouse, you need to make sure that you have chosen the type of greenhouse that you are going to build. This will make the rest of the decisions that you are about to make it much easier. Make sure you look back at the information that we covered in the last chapter to choose the type of greenhouse that is perfect for you.

Next, you will need to choose where your greenhouse will be located. Typically, the south side of your home is the best place to put a greenhouse. This is because it will get the best and most sunlight in this location. Be sure when choosing your location, though, that there will be nothing that blocks the sun from reaching your greenhouse. For example, if your yard is bordered by tall trees and the south side of your property never sees the sun, then your property is an exception from the fact that the south side is typically the best for greenhouses. If you do not have space on the south side, it is also okay to choose a different location. You want to ensure that you get to create a perfect greenhouse—no matter what its location is. The most important thing to consider is that the space receives a decent amount of direct sunlight throughout the day.

You also need to figure out how big you want your greenhouse to be. You will want to think about the big picture while you are making this choice. How many plants you would like to grow this year is one thing to consider, but you will also want to think about how many plants you could see yourself growing ten years down the road. You will probably want to build your greenhouse big enough to fit your dream garden so that later on you do not have to regret making it too small. You also need to consider the space that you have available when you are making this decision. Do you have enough space in your designated location for a large greenhouse or do you need to build a structure that is on the smaller side? Do you want to take up your entire designated space with the greenhouse or would you like to leave some outdoor area to enjoy as well? When you look into answering these questions for yourself, you should be able to decide how big you would like the greenhouse that you are building to be.

Now that we know the basics of the greenhouse structure and its location, it is time for us to move our planning inside. The inside of your greenhouse needs to create the perfect environment for the plants that you are most wanting to grow. Because of this, when you are planning the interior of your greenhouse, you will be looking mostly into its functionality. You certainly can plan the looks of the inside of your structure, but this is nowhere near as important as how well it performs.

Let's start looking into how to design the inside of your greenhouse in a practical and functional way by looking at air flow. Airflow is needed to ensure that the plants get what they need. Plants breathe in a way that is the opposite of humans. Humans breathe in oxygen and out carbon dioxide. Humans need fresh air to supply oxygen where they are breathing, because breathing back in the carbon dioxide that they breathed out will do no good for sustaining life. This same principle is true with plants. Plants need carbon dioxide in the air so that they can breathe it in. When they breathe out, they release oxygen. Oxygen is not good for sustaining the life of the plants. Because of this, the air in greenhouses needs to be circulated just like it is naturally outside so that plants are breathing in the things that they actually need in order for them to survive.

Airflow in greenhouses is achieved mainly through the use of fans. There are quite a few options based on types of fans and the location of fans that you will need to plant out, however. Each of these options comes with its own specific set of benefits. You will need to decide what will work best in your structure and for the plants that you are most wanting to grow.

You can arrange your fans in something called a parallel layout, which means that all of the fans are on the same side of the greenhouse and lined up parallel to each other. When they are turned on, they blow the air in the same direction which causes the air to circulate around the whole greenhouse. This method for fans is best in areas that are on flat land as it does not work well with hills.

If your greenhouse is on hilly land, you may benefit more from a fan arrangement called the series method. This is an arrangement of fans that starts at the outside of the greenhouse and moves toward the middle. It again helps to move the air in a circular motion around the greenhouse structure.

Next, let's look into the different types of fans that you can choose from. The first type of fan that is commonly found in greenhouses is called a basket fan. Basket fans are very powerful and have wide slots. They are strong fans, so they are able to circulate air well, but when they are used in sequences, they do not always provide a uniform stream of air. This can cause some plants to get a lot of airflow and others to get none at all.

Shrouded fans are an option as well. They are able to provide more consistent air flow to all plants. They are also great for conserving energy, so if you are looking to "go green" with your greenhouse, shrouded fans could be a great choice.

After you choose a fan type, you will have to decide if you want your air flow to be vertical or horizontal. Both methods have their good points and not so good points. Vertical air flow, for example, helps to ensure that the temperature of the greenhouse stays even throughout the entire structure from top to bottom. Horizontal airflow is better at making sure that the humidity levels are consistent among every area of plants in the greenhouse.

Next, let's look into cooling and heating. We know that these are two of the most important factors to look into when designing a new greenhouse. The purpose of a greenhouse is actually to extend the growing season of your plants and your garden, and one of the biggest ways that they can do this is through temperature control. When you can control the temperature of your greenhouse, you do not need to rely on the natural climate in your area for the health and success of your plants. Let's look into some things that you can do to your greenhouse so that you are able to control the temperature well.

First, let's look into greenhouse heating techniques. One of the simplest ways to make sure that your greenhouse stays warm is to make sure that it is built well. Make sure that it is in a location that gets a lot of sunlight and that it is made from a material that allows heat to enter inside. You can also make sure that your greenhouse has no cracks that could let breezes of cold air come in.

If you live in an extremely cold climate, you may need to consider some more heating techniques. You could use a greenhouse heater to apply heat inside your structure. You could also consider using solar panels on top of your greenhouse to collect energy for heat so that you could continue along the environmentally friendly path that your greenhouse idea started.

When you live in a cold area, you will need to plant for these things during the design process. Consider installing a heater or solar panels right away so that your plants are never hurt by painfully cold temperatures.

If you live in a climate that gets extremely hot during certain seasons, you may actually need to find ways to cool it down. The first thing to try when your greenhouse begins to get too warm is to cool it down with the fans that you use for air circulation. If this does not work, you could consider some sort of ventilation in your walls. If this also does not work, you can buy a cover for your greenhouse to give your plants a break from the heat that the sun provides them with.

When designing your greenhouse, you will want to make sure that you have the option to use these methods if you live in a very warm climate. You can consider walls that can be rolled up partially to allow for ventilation. You'll want to make sure that your design includes fans. You may even want to consider having a cover ready for the days that you know your greenhouse will get too much sun and therefore too much heat.

Next, let's look at the humidity in your greenhouse. If your greenhouse is too humid, you will want to make sure that you are using the horizontal fan method. This helps to circulate the air directly around the plants so that the humidity does not sit in them for too long. Another way to design your greenhouse so that humidity is never an issue is to have flooring that drains well. This will make sure that there is never excess water in your greenhouse that could lead to too much humidity in the air.

The flooring of your greenhouse is also important. As we mentioned earlier, it is important to have floor drains if you think that humidity is going to be a problem because of the climate that you live in. Besides this, though, there are many things to keep in mind when choosing a greenhouse flooring material. Let's look into the different types of materials that are commonly used in greenhouse flooring as well as what each different choice is good for.

Next, let's look into the different types of greenhouse floors as well as what each different type is good for. One popular flooring type for a greenhouse is concrete. Concrete is easy to walk on and easy to keep clean. It is also easy to slope so that you can get good drainage in your building. To have a concrete floor, you will probably have to have a concrete slab made before you build your greenhouse.

You can also have gravel for the inside of your greenhouse. This is typically done with weed cloth so that weeds do not grow through the bottom of your flooring. The gravel is then dumped on top of that and is a few inches thick. This is a good choice if you want a more natural look. It is also a good choice if you want the option of adding extra humidity because you can spray the flooring with water and the extra water will not be slippery, but it will also stick around so that it is able to add to the humidity in your greenhouse.

Similar to the gravel flooring, some people also have landscape rock as flooring inside of their greenhouse. This has all of the same benefits that the gravel flooring has, it is just a little fancier and a little better looking.

You could also choose to make your floor out of brick. This again makes a really sturdy base similar to the concrete flooring, but it also allows for added humidity similar to the rock and gravel flooring. Brick floors are also very sturdy and lasts a long time.

If you are on a tight budget, you could choose to make a floor out of mulch in your greenhouse. Mulch is not the best greenhouse floor because you cannot clean it. It works well and is fine to walk on, but you will need to replace it as soon as it gets dirty or too wet. You do not want the mulch floor in your greenhouse to introduce near your plants.

There are also some companies who sell greenhouse flooring. These words can be made of materials like rubber. These floors are often really nice to have because they are made specifically for greenhouses. They are typically easy to walk on and drain well. The downside of them as they may be expensive as they are made specifically for greenhouses and nothing else.

Will also want to look into the glazing that you use for your greenhouse. Glazing is the material that covers the outside of your greenhouse. It is the plastic, or glass, or polycarbonate material that keeps your plants safe, keeps the temperature warm and humidity in, and overall makes your structure the greenhouse that it is. Choosing the right type of glazing is an important choice, so let's look into the different options and what their biggest benefits are.

First, let's look into the glass as a glazing material. Glass is a nice material because it is strong and lasts a long time. It only ever breaks down or needs replacing if it breaks. It also does a good job of letting light in. However, it has some downsides as well. It is really expensive to replace as if the glass on your greenhouse brakes you basically have to just pay for it all to be replaced again. It also allows direct light to go straight into your plants and does not diffuse the light as it enters, so it's not as good for your plans as other types of glazing that allow for diffusion of light.

Next, let's look into polycarbonate. Polycarbonate glazing is strong, and it allows for light to be diffused as it enters into the greenhouse. This is really good for the plants that you are growing. It is a durable material, and it lasts a long time. However, it has the downside of having to be treated with deliberately every once in a while so that it keeps its nice color and functionality.

The last type of glazing that we will look into is called the poly film. A poly film is a cheap option for glazing, which makes it a great option for many people who are on a tight budget. It works best in warm climates because it is not the best insulator. It does, however, work well if you do not need your greenhouse to the insulated extremely well. Sadly, it does not last as long as the other materials either. It is basically just a good choice if you need something cheap for the time being while you wait to get something nicer later on.

Next, let's look into the safety and security of your greenhouse. If you choose to have a greenhouse that is made of lightweight materials, you would need to make sure that it is safe in the wind. To do this, you will need to think about using greenhouse stakes. You can put these stakes through the corners of your lightweight material and into the ground. This will help to keep your greenhouse from blowing away in inclement weather.

Overall, it is clear that there are a lot of things to keep in mind when you are choosing how to build your greenhouse. There are even more things to keep in mind when you are looking into the inside of your greenhouse and the functionality that it will need to have. You will need to look into the temperature that your greenhouse will need to be as well as how to allow that to happen. You will need to figure out how to keep the humidity levels where you need them to be. You will need to look into heat and cooling. You will need to look into the floor that it drains well and that it is the material that you prefer. You will need to look into glazing and choose which material is best for what you can afford. You will also need to make sure that your greenhouses safe and secure and inclement weather. If you keep all of this in mind while you are designing a greenhouse, you will end up with a greenhouse that works well for you in any situation.

CHAPTER FOUR
Greenhouse Essentials

Congratulations! You have gotten through the hard part of planning your greenhouse. You have figured out the structure that you want to use. You know where you are going to put your greenhouse. You know what it's going to look like on the inside and what features you needed to have so that it can function well. Next, let's start looking at some of the fun stuff. Let's look into greenhouse essentials. These are added features that you can put into your greenhouse to allow it to do every purpose that you needed to do. These features can help you to optimize your plant growth and health.

One fun greenhouse essential is an irrigation system. An irrigation system is a device that water's your plans for you. It is typically a set of tubing or hoses that runs throughout your greenhouse near all of your plans. It has things that are almost like mini sprinklers on it. These little sprinklers go off at certain times of the day, scheduled by you, to water your plants. You can set them up to water your plants for a certain amount of time. For example, you could tell them to start spraying water for 5 minutes straight. You can also tell them when to turn on. For example, you could tell them to turn on five times a day. In some cases, you could even tell them which five times a day you would like this to be. For example, you could tell them that you want them to turn on at 5 a.m., 8 a.m., 11 a.m., 2 p.m., and 5 p.m. They are a customizable machine that can save you a lot of time when you would have been watering your plants for hours each day though.

Irrigation systems are cool because they allow you to set up how much water to give to your plants. It's not like a simple sprinkler that turns on, and you need to remember to turn it off when your plant has had too much. You can turn it on to only spray a little bit for your tropical plants, or you can turn it on to completely soak your vegetables. It's customizable and can fit your goals with any type of plant that you have.

Irrigation systems can also be very environmentally friendly. This is because they are very precise with their watering and they do not waste much water. They can add to your conservation efforts to help you to save water. They can help make your greenhouse even more "green."

Another essential that you may need to have in your greenhouses lighting. Typically, greenhouses provide all of the access that a plant needs through the sun. However, if your greenhouse is not in the location where it gets enough sun or if you have plans that need excess sun during a time of year where your area of the world does not get much done at all, you might need your own nights.

The type of lights that you will need to buy depends on the type of plants that you are boring. For example, there are certain types of plant lights that are made specifically for growing flowers. There are other types of plant lights that are made specifically for growing seedlings.

And that you know how to pick the right type of light for your plant. Not all lights are the same. You cannot just take out light bulbs from your kitchen lamp and put it in your greenhouse. This will not help your plants to grow. You need "grow lights" to help your plants to your best ability. Let's look into these lights, how they work, and what you should know before you buy them below.

Let's look into fluorescent lights. Fluorescent lights are the lights that you typically see in stores or schools, so they may look familiar to you. They are a good choice for people who own homes and have their greenhouses on their property because they are energy efficient and should not make the electric bill go up to high. They are made up with a blue light, which makes them good for growing seeds. They also do not get very hot, so they are able to be placed right next to the seeds, and they will not be able to burn them.

HID, or high-intensity discharge lights, are a common trait as well. These are very bright lights that can help a lot of plants grow at the same time. They work best in large greenhouses with high ceilings. This is because they can help a lot of plants at the same time and because they should be placed high above the plants because they get hot and you do not want them to burn your plants.

A lot of people use high-pressure sodium lights in their greenhouses as well. These are another type of HID lights. These lights have a positive note of lasting a long time, but they have the negative note of not being the best for your plants. This is because they are closer to the website of the light spectrum and not the blue side. This makes them not as good for growing plants as other lights that are closer to the blue side of the spectrum.

With all of these options, you should be able to choose what type of light to design your greenhouse with. This information shows you which lights are good for which causes, and how far away they should be placed from the plants. If you are greenhouse does not have adequate sunlight, or if you live in a climate that goes through times of the year that the sun is not out for long, you may want to consider some of these light choices.

The thing that is essential to your success in growing inside of your greenhouse is shelving. You also want to plan and design your shelving so that you are able to use it to its best ability. Later in the book, we will look into shelving and how to use the space in your greenhouse creatively, but for now, let's just look into it a little bit.

You will need to choose what type of shelving you would like to use in your greenhouse. You can use resin as shelving if you want something that is durable, plastic, and long-lasting. You can choose to use wood shelves if you want to build something yourself. You could also choose to use metal shelves for something that is sturdy. You want to make sure that your shelves are sturdy, durable and that they will not tip over. If they are tipping, you might want to secure them to the wall or to the ground. It would be really sad if a shelf tipped over and all of your plans were lost. Because of this, you need to take your shelving seriously and make sure that it is the best type of shelving for your space. You will want to have shelves that fit in your space and allow you to optimize the use of your space as well.

You may also want to have some sort of natural pest control as a greenhouse essential. This does not have to be chemicals, especially if you are looking to keep your greenhouse and your garden organic in nature. You could use a sheet of mash near the door to make sure that no bugs follow you in when you come into the greenhouse. This would be a good way to keep bugs outside so that you do not have to worry about chemicals later on down the road if your plants happened to be infested by bugs.

Another greenhouse essential that is small but something that you really need and that is something that you might forget about, is a thermometer. You will always want to know how warm your plants are. This will help you to be able to allow them to be successful. It will help you to know if they are too hot or too cold and if you need to add extra heating or cooling efforts to your greenhouse. Make sure that when you are designing your greenhouse, you have a thermometer right away. This will help you from avoiding many unnecessary struggles with temperature and plants along the road.

Are designing your greenhouse, you may also want to think about how you are going to clean it. Especially if your windows are made of glass, they will look dirty really fast. You also do not want your greenhouse to get dirty or moldy because you want your plants to say how the inside of it. You also do not want it to get dirty because you want it to last a long time and you want to treat your new creation for a while. Because of this, while you are designing your greenhouse, you might want to consider having an area for your cleaning supplies or creating a cleaning kit to have inside. This could include things that will help to clean your windows, your walls, or your floors. It could help to make sure your shelves are clean. These efforts will not only protect rain house, but they could help protect your plants from diseases, molds, and bacteria as well.

Another really simple thing that you might forget about is containers. Containers are what you are going to be growing most of your plants in. When you are growing in a garden inside a greenhouse, you will need an assortment of different sized containers for your different size plants. You may want small containers for planting seeds. You may want larger containers for your larger plants. You may want trays for plants that are litter-related or can go near each other. You will want to make sure that your containers that you pick outfit on your shelves and that they look nice in your greenhouse so that your overall look can be aesthetically pleasing.

Another greenhouse essential may be a specific place to plant your plants. Potting plants can take up a lot of space. It can be a messy process when you start to involve soil and seeds. Because of this, you might want to have a special place to do it. This will keep you from having to plant plants inside of your house. It will avoid a lot of unnecessary messes. Because of this, you may want to have a bench or table where you can start your plants whenever you need to. This could even have a little storage space to keep extra containers, seeds, or soil if you have enough space to do so. It could really make your greenhouse into a perfect growing and gardening atmosphere. It could allow you to have everything you need to start plants and see them through all the way until harvest inside one small building.

We mentioned this earlier a little bit when we were talking about cooling your greenhouse, but another greenhouse essential could be shading covers. You need a shade cover when it is a hot summer day and when your plants are getting too much sun. Without this, your plants could actually die from getting too much direct sunlight or too much heat. You do not want to allow this to happen. To avoid this, you could have shade covers ready from the moment you design your greenhouse. You could have a special place to keep them, or you could have some sort of shade cover that is already attached and just needed to be stretched out to cover the top of your greenhouse. With this added essential, you will be protected from one of the easiest ways to lose plants in a greenhouse.

Another greenhouse essential that you will want to make sure you have a Spence. This kind of goes back to structure, but it is a little thing that you need to remember to have. It might be something that you forget when you are looking at the big picture, but it is very important—so let's look into it. You want to have vents so that your plants can get the air that they need to. Vents can help with both cooling and air circulation. Cooling and air circulation are both extremely important in the life of plants in a greenhouse. If plants get too hot, they will not make it. If plants do not get enough carbon dioxide to breathe in, they also will not make it. Because of this, but can be a huge tool and keeping your plants alive. Make sure that you have vents in the walls of a greenhouse that you can open and close. You do not want them to be open all the time because that may make them major greenhouse cold in the winter. You will want them to open and shut, and you will want them to be a part of your greenhouse right away in its first design.

Overall, you can see that greenhouses have many essential pieces. You have a lot to think about when you are designing a greenhouse. The things that you have to think about do not stop with the outer structure or even with the indoor design. They lead to you needing to think about the little things that you need to have ready inside of your greenhouse. These things can be a part of the structure like the vents that we just talked about, or they can be something as little as a cleaning kit. No matter what these essentials are, they are all equally important. You need to make sure that you were thinking about things like irrigation systems, lighting, and even space to do things like planting seeds. If you include all of these essentials into your greenhouse, you will have the perfect space where you can do everything you need to do and where your plants can survive and succeed. These essentials will create the perfect greenhouse atmosphere for you to design.

CHAPTER FIVE
Maximizing Your Greenhouse Space

Now that we have looked into everything that you will need to make your greenhouse the perfect environment based on your space and climate and for your favorite plants let's look into how you can maximize the space inside of it. This is especially important if you have a small greenhouse that you are planning to build in the small space that you have available. It is important for bug greenhouses as well, though. No matter how big your greenhouse is going to be, you more than likely want to fit as many plants as possible inside of it. There are a few different things that you can do to make sure that you are using every little bit of space that your greenhouse can give you.

One of the most important tips in making sure that you will be able to use every space that your greenhouse has to offer is to plan ahead. You need to know how you are planning on making this work before you start. That way, if there are certain benches that will work better to plant on, for example, you can get the correct ones from the start. It will also help because you will know that a space-saving greenhouse has been your goal all along, so you will not need to reframe your thinking on your interior greenhouse design.

One way to maximize the growing space in your greenhouse is by using movable benches or shelving units. If your benches or shelves are moveable, you can actually plant in up to ninety percent of the space inside of your greenhouse. This works by only leaving enough space for one aisle to walk through the inside of your greenhouse, and the rest of the space is completely filled with plants. You then move the shelves or benches in order to get to other areas of the greenhouse. This can make your plant care a little more time consuming, but the added growing space can be worth the extra effort.

You could also consider having two sets of different leveled benches to plant on. One set would be a typical height and would stay in place at all times. The other would be on wheels. It would be shorter, and it would be able to roll right under the other bench.

In this system, you would roll the lower bench out into the aisle during the day so that it could get adequate sunlight. You would then roll it back underneath at night or whenever you needed to walk throughout the greenhouse.

You can also maximize the space in your greenhouse that you are able to use for planting by using the floor space that you have available. Typically, the floor space in greenhouses is just empty and almost wasted space. If you place plants all around the floor, you will be able to almost double your growing space while giving a function to that previously purposeless space.

Similar to using the floor space, you can use the space above your plants as well. To use this space, you could install hanging rods toward the top of your greenhouse. You could then use these rods to grow plants inside of hanging baskets. This would allow you to use the space in the air above your plants that were previously completely empty. It is another way to maximize the use of every space inside of your greenhouse.

It is not only hanging pots that can maximize the use of your vertical space, however. There are many tools available on today's market that allow you to partake in what is called vertical gardening. Vertical gardening maximizes vertical space. It is extremely popular for people who want to have large gardens but do not have much space. These same tools and ideas can be used inside of your greenhouse. You can use special shelving techniques, pot holders, and more to make sure that you are maximizing your vertical space as much as you possibly can.

When you are maximizing your vertical space, however, there is something that you need to look out for. You need to make sure that all of your plants are still getting adequate lighting. You do not want to place vertical gardening tools or potholders in places that will cause them to block the sun that the plants that you have growing on your benches will need. If you really need to use your vertical space but find yourself blocking a lot of much-needed sunlight, you could consider adding additional lighting inside of your greenhouse to make sure that all of your plants are getting all of the sunshine that they need to grow and thrive.

You could even consider something called under bench production. It is the process of growing plants under the benches that hold your other plants on top of them. This process is not like the moveable benches because these plants really never need to come out. To grow plants in this area, you would need to have extra lighting underneath your benches. The lighting would need to be a variety that can be close to growing plants because there would not be a lot of space available between the lights and the plants when they are already confined to a certain space underneath a bench.

Another way to make sure that you are maximizing your growing space inside of your greenhouse is to ensure that you have chosen the right type of container to grow in. If you choose containers that do not work well together on benches, you might be losing growing space. If you choose containers that have too much space for the plant that is inside of them, you could be losing growing space from this choice as well. When you choose what type of growing containers to use, you will want to make sure that they are both the right size for the plants that will be in them and that they sit nicely next to each other on the benches so that no unused space is left in between containers. Typically, square containers that are made for planting work well for this. Trays are also a good choice since they basically turn the whole bench into a planting space so that no space is lost to container edges at all.

Crop scheduling can be a good tool for not only your production but for your greenhouse space maximization as well. If you are scheduling your crops, you know when one plant will be ready to harvested and when it will need to be replaced by a new seedling. This is an extremely helpful tool in seeds that only produce one crop like celery. If you know when your celery will be ready, you can have a new seedling ready to replace it in its same spot. This will help you not to have to lose space to the new group of crops, and it will immediately help you know how to fill the hole that your harvest just created.

Greenhouse zoning can help you to maximize your space as well. Typically staging is used as a convenience to the gardener and an organization tool, but it'll definitely benefit the amount of growing space that you have available as well. When you are zoning plants, you will want to put them near other plants that have the same needs as them. For example, if you have five types of plants that need the same strong light on for many hours of the day, you will want to place them next to each other. This gives you extra space because it allows you to press all of those plants close to each other under the one lamp. If you have them spread out, you would probably end up having to give each separate plat their own light as well as some extra empty space so that the light would not shine on plants that would be hurt by it. By allowing you to place all of the plants close together and making sure the light touches them but no other plants that do not need it, you will save quite a bit of space from going unused.

Overall, it is clear that there are a lot of different ways to maximize the space inside of your greenhouse. As we mentioned earlier, it is important to maximize your space if you have a small greenhouse, but also if you have a large one as well. You do not want to have to miss out on any available growing space. When you are planning out how to use your growing space to its full potential, come back to this chapter for ideas and information. You can maximize your space through things like benches, organization plans, and zoning. You can use your vertical space by planting in hanging devices and by planting on the floor. You can ensure that you have great space saving containers and trays and you can be ready to plan your crops. All of these things will allow you to plant as much as your greenhouse can possibly hold. These things will help you to get the most out of the structure that you are planning to build.

CHAPTER SIX
Seasonal Preparation and Care

The main reason why you are building a greenhouse is probably that you want to extend your growing season. In order to do this, there are a few things that you will need to do. When a new season comes, you will need to prepare your greenhouse to help the plants inside of it succeed. In this chapter, we are going to look into everything that you have to do to prepare your greenhouse for the upcoming season. This information will allow you to use your greenhouse in the way that you plan to use it. If you can make sure your greenhouses ready for every season, you can ensure that your plans will have success no matter what the temperature is outside.

First, let's look into what you need to do to winterize your greenhouse. We are going to start in winter because it is the most common season that people use greenhouses for. This is because, in most areas of the world, winter is not the best time to grow plants outside in the garden. It is, however, a great time to grow inside of a greenhouse if you know how to winterize your structure.

The first thing that you will want to do is make sure your greenhouse is clean and ready for the winter. Winter is not a great time to be opening doors or taking a lot of trips in and out of your greenhouse. In the winter, you don't want the cold air to enter when you walk into your greenhouse, so you should make sure that you were going in and out as little as possible and as fast as possible. Because of this, you want to make sure that your greenhouses all ready for the winter before the winter comes. That way, you don't have to be moving shelves in and out, taking plants in and out, or anything else that will cost you to open the door more than you need to.

Cleaning your greenhouse may not be the first thing that you think of when you start the process of winterizing, but it is the most important thing to start with. Because, after you begin the other winterizing methods that you will need to do, you will already be done with the simple stuff. If you think that you will have to rearrange your greenhouse or take anything in and out of it, this is the most important place to start.

Next, you will want to make sure that there are no places in your greenhouse that could allow cold air to get inside. You will want to look at the walls and make sure that there are no holes. If there are holes in the wall, you will want to patch them. You will even need to look at your windows and doorways during this process. You will need to make sure that your door is lined up correctly so that it cannot allow cold air through cracks that may be around their edges. You will want to make sure that any of your windows are shut tight. You may want to check on the ground of your greenhouse to make sure there are no cracks or gaps as well. If you see cracks are gaps in any of these spaces, you will need to cover them.

If your greenhouse has vents that allow for additional air circulation in the summer, you will want to make sure that these are closed or covered as well. If your vents do not close tightly, you can cover them with a plastic window treatment to make sure no cold air will be able to seep through its holes.

If you live in a particularly cold area, you may need a heater inside of your greenhouse to keep your plants healthy in the winter. You will know if your greenhouse needs a heater if the sun is not enough to keep your plants warm during the colder months. If this is something that you will need, it is important that you get your heater set up and make sure that it is working well before the cold air hits your area. You do not want your plants to be affected by a freeze before you have the chance to protect them with the heater.

When you are thinking of how you are going to heat your greenhouse, make sure that you remember to keep in mind the size of your structure. If you have a large greenhouse, some heating systems may not be able to provide enough warmth to cover your entire large space. Make sure that you are able to check how much square footage the heater will cover and that it matches up to the square footage that your greenhouse has before you decide to purchase the device.

If you heat your greenhouse in the winter, it is also a good idea to think about having a backup heating option. If your power goes out one night, you do not want to have to lose all of your plants just because you were not completely prepared for the things that could go wrong. You could consider having a battery powered back up heating system in case struggles like this ever does appear.

Aside from heaters, you can also help to keep your greenhouse warm through the use of insulation. If your greenhouse is insulated well, not as much cold air will be able to get inside of it. How do you insulate a greenhouse that has to have walls thin enough to allow the sunlight through, though? You can use certain linings on your greenhouse walls that help to reflect light and heat. These will help to keep warm air in and cold air out.

One important thing to remember when you are winterizing your greenhouse is just because it is cold outside does not mean that your plants do not need fresh air. You still need to use fans to circulate the air in your greenhouse and ventilation is necessary to some level, even in the cold. This is because plants cannot survive solely on the oxygen that they breathe back out into the air. They need carbon dioxide as well. If they breathe up the carbon dioxide in the greenhouse and they are not given any fresh air, they will not have what they need in order to survive.

When the long, cold winter ends, you will need to start preparing your garden for spring. This may at first feel like you are just undoing everything that you did to winterize your greenhouse, but it is much more than that, and it is very important to the health of your plants and the success of your crops.

When spring comes, you may want to start your preparation in the same way that we started the winter preparation; cleaning. Typically, greenhouses are taken care of less during the winter mainly because the big focus of the gardeners is to keep the plants warm, not really to keep it looking nice. You can start by making sure that your greenhouse is clean, anything that you no longer wish to use is removed, and the setup is what you would like to see it stay as throughout the next growing season.

You will then want to make sure that your plants are getting lots of fresh air once again. Make sure that the fans are up and running well, uncover or open up all of the vents, and even open up the windows if you have them. A long winter with minimal fresh air is hard on plants, so giving them some clean air is an important step in the spring preparation process.

After getting your greenhouse ready for spring, you will need to start thinking about summer. Your spring greenhouse should work the same as your summer greenhouse unless you need to use certain types of cooling techniques. You could consider using a shade cover on your greenhouse. This would be a good thing to get ready before the sun gets too hot so that you are prepared when the time actually comes when you need to use it.

After summer, you will need to start preparing for fall. For fall preparation, you will basically just be starting to think about your winterization techniques. Make sure that you are ready early in case winter decides to show up sooner than it is expected.

Overall, there are different types of preparations that you will need to do for every season of the year. These preparations will allow you to keep your greenhouse as the perfect environment for your plants and their success throughout the entire year. There is a very large amount of work to do to prepare your greenhouse for winter, but preparations for the other three seasons requires minimal work. If you follow these guidelines while you are getting your greenhouse ready for each season, you should be able to keep your plants happy and healthy all year long.

PART TWO
Growing in Your Greenhouse

CHAPTER SEVEN
What to Plant in Your Greenhouse

We have talked about everything you need to know in order to build your greenhouse. We've talked about the structure as well as the interior. We've talked about everything that you need in order to allow your greenhouse to be the perfect environment for your plants. We've talked about how to maximize the space in your greenhouse, and we've even talked about how you can prepare your greenhouse for the different seasons of the year. Now, it's time to look at the reason why you are building a greenhouse. In this chapter, we are going to learn about the different types of plants that you can grow in a greenhouse. We will look at fruits, vegetables, herbs, tropical plants, and hydroponics.

First, let's look at fruits. You can grow fruits in a variety of ways in a greenhouse. You can grow them in containers or tray, and you can also grow entire trees inside of greenhouses. Growing fruit trees is not probably something that you think about when you think about greenhouses and what can be grown inside of them. However, greenhouses were actually created to grow orange trees inside them. They used to be called orangeries. Orangeries were made so that oranges could be found throughout the entire year in areas of the world that have cold weather such as England.

You can grow fruit trees in your greenhouse today just as well as people used to when they were still called or injuries. In order to grow fruit trees in your greenhouse, you want your greenhouse to be warm and humid. You will want to make sure that the temperature never goes below 50 degrees and that you are watering your plants often. You could even consider using a misting system as fruit trees like light watering in short intervals. Growing fruit trees inside of greenhouses is a fun option because a lot of areas in the world are areas that fruit trees cannot be grown at all if they are outside. Greenhouses make it possible for people who live in these areas to grow the trees of their own.

If you are not looking to grow an entire fruit tree and wants an easier and more commonly used option, you can grow fruit plants like strawberries as well. Growing fruit plants inside of greenhouses is an easy way to gain nutritious fruits for you and your family all year long. They can be grown in greenhouses just like they're growing outside. It's often even easier to grow food in greenhouses than it is from an outdoor garden because wild animals love them, and wild animals are not able to get your fruits when they are grown in a greenhouse.

From fruit trees and small plants, you can also grow fruit bushes. This allows you to grow plants like blueberries, raspberries, and blackberries. You can grow this in a greenhouse fairly easily. They do take up more space than a small plant like strawberry would, because they are tall and need large containers for their long roots. However, you are able to fit them in many different sized greenhouses pretty easily. To fit them best, you can consider not putting them on the shelf at all. Since bushes are tall, you can put them right on the ground, and they would still be had a good harvest level for you.

Overall, if you are looking to grow fruit in a greenhouse, you have many ways to do it, and most of the ways are pretty simple. You can grow fruit with trees, bushes, or plants. All you will need to be able to do this is a warm greenhouse with a good humidity level; this is really easy to achieve through sunshine and watering your plants often.

Oh, let's look into growing vegetables in a greenhouse. Vegetables are one of the most commonly found things pro greenhouses. They are easy to grow in small spaces. They are also easy to grow in containers. This makes them great for growing on bunches in a small space like a greenhouse. They're also commonly grown in greenhouses because they provide food for you and your family. A lot of people grow vegetables to cut back on their grocery bill or two just to introduce more natural and healthy foods into their lives and onto their dinner plates. Because of this, vegetables are a great option for plants to grow in your greenhouse. Let's look into some of the different vegetable types that you may want to grow inside of your house as well as some tips that will help you to do so.

First, you will want to know when choosing vegetables that there are cool season vegetables and warm season vegetables. You can either choose to have cool season vegetables and keep your greenhouse a little bit colder or warm season vegetables and keep your greenhouse a little bit warmer. You can also choose to have both and simply give the warm season vegetables a little bit more light than the cold seasoned vegetables need. You can do this through the use of light bulbs and artificial lighting. Vegetables like lettuce and broccoli are considered cool seasoned vegetables and vegetables like peppers and cucumbers are considered warm season vegetables.

However, pretty much any type of vegetable can be planted in a greenhouse. Vegetables that are easy to plant in small containers include tomatoes, peppers, broccoli, lettuce, spinach, kale, peas, carrots, radishes, and cucumbers. Vegetables are good for small spaces and are fine with staying in a container their entire lives. Vegetables that we need bigger containers to enclose them in are plants like potatoes because these grow underground and take up a lot of space.

You can also choose to grow a vegetable garden inside a greenhouse and later transplanted to be outside. If you do this, you will want to start your vegetables and smoke tanners in the greenhouse. You can start your vegetables when the weather is still too cold for outdoor gardening. The best time to start these vegetables is in early spring. This will allow your vegetables to be the right size to transfer once the ground is warm enough to plant them outside. You will not want to plant your seedlings outside until the ground does not freeze anymore. If there is still a chance of a hard frost happening in the future, you will not want to put them outside yet. This is because this hard frost could kill your plans. So, it is best to keep your seedlings in your greenhouse for as long as possible.

Once you move busy things outside, they will be able to grow just fine in the ground. However, not all seeds can be transmitted to be grown outside. See you like carrots should not be transplanted. This is because once the carrots start growing, they need to stay in the same place. If you want them or transplant them, they will come out of the ground in odd shapes. They can even sometimes not survive the transplant. Plants that are easy to transplant include tomatoes, peppers, cucumbers, celery, kale, onions, and eggplant.

What to transplant your seeds to an outdoor garden, you can grow vegetables in your greenhouse and keep them there until it is harvest time as well. To do this, you will want to make sure that your containers are big enough to hold the entire plant. For example, you do not want to grow a tomato plant in a 3in by 3in container, when you know that it will soon be too big for this. You want to make sure that the containers that you use are able to support the adult version of the plant. You will also want to make sure that there is adequate space in your greenhouse. Growing vegetables and harvesting them inside of your greenhouse will take up more space than going simply sweet thanks. It is still a great option to grow vegetables and be able to harvest them all year long, however—even if it does come with its difficulties.

Overall, vegetables are a great thing to grow in a greenhouse. You can grow them to transport them to the garden, or you can grow them to harvest inside of the greenhouse. You can grow many different types of vegetables, and you can use this hobby to add a lot of nutritious ingredients to the dinner table in your home. Growing vegetables is easy, and it is rewarding. With the information in this section, you should be able to figure out what temperature to keep your greenhouse app for certain vegetables, and you should be able to look through some ideas and find out if you want to grow any vegetables in your own greenhouse.

Another thing that you can grow in a greenhouse is herbs. Herbs are a good thing to grow because they are something that you can use in a lot of meals. They are also fairly small and can be grown in small spaces. This means that they will not take up much space in your big greenhouse. It also means that they are a great thing to be grown in a smaller greenhouse such as a cold frame or a window greenhouse.

If you want to go something in a Cold Frame greenhouse, herbs are a great choice. They are a great choice because you do not need very many Arabs in order to have enough to cook for you and your family. You only need to use a little bit of time, so having one plant of each herb is plenty for most people. If you want to grow herbs on a bigger scale, you can grow them in your bigger greenhouse. Growing a lot of herbs in a large greenhouse would typically mean that you would want to sell them because there is not watch that people can do with large amounts of herbs.

Now that we know why you would want to grow herbs in your greenhouse, let's look into how to do it. The process of growing herbs in your greenhouse is very similar to growing vegetables in your greenhouse. Herbs are easy to grow, and they do well in greenhouses.

The most important thing to know when you are growing herbs in your greenhouse is to make sure that they are getting out of the water. The most common reason that Arabs do not survive when people try to grow them is that they are not watered often enough. Herbs are not plants that like to be drenched in water. They like to be constantly missed it with small amounts of water. Because of this, if you want to grow herbs in your greenhouse, it might be a good idea to install a misting system. If you do not have a misting system, you will have to be outside watering your herbs many times a day. You could also consider installing a dripping system, which can be much cheaper than a misting system. A dripping system is simply a container our machine that drips water down onto your plants. This allows the plants to get a small amount of water at a time and it helps the humidity in the greenhouse to rise.

Another thing to consider when you want to grow herbs in your greenhouses that herbs do not like all day sunshine. Herbs do best when they are grown in places that have adequate amounts of shade. Because of this, if you want to grow herbs in your greenhouse, you will probably need to install a shade on top of your structure. This shade will allow your herbs to get the amount of shade that they need well still getting the heat that they need from the sun.

Some great herbs to grow in a greenhouse include basil, cilantro, chives, parsley, and dill. These herbs are actually pretty sensitive and are hard to grow in an outdoor garden. Because of this, people love to grow them and greenhouses. Greenhouses are actually one of the main places that these types of herbs survive well.

You can also grow mint in a greenhouse. However, it is important to know that mint is an invasive plant. Because it is invasive, mint should be planted in a container and should not be planted near other plans. You do not want you to take over the other plants and kill them. However, if you grow mint correctly, it can be a great plant for you to have.

Overall, it is easy to see that a greenhouse is a great place to grow arms. It takes plants that are typically hard to grow and give a perfect atmosphere. It takes plants that also do not take up much space, and give some the perfect place to be grown. Herbs can be grown in greenhouses as small as windows or cold frames and in a bag of greenhouses as our bill today. They are very versatile, and their harvest can benefit many meals people enjoy eating today. Because of all these factors, herbs are a great thing to consider growing in your greenhouse.

If you are looking to grow something other than food, tropical plants can be a great thing to grow in greenhouses. Tropical plants are typically only able to be grown in warm climates. They are beautiful, however, so people in colder climates are often jealous of these majestic plants. Often times, people in colder climates actually even grow these plants in the summer months and then let them die in the winter because they cannot handle the cold, but they still want to be able to enjoy the beauty of them when they are able to survive. If you grow these tropical plants in greenhouses, however, you are able to keep them alive all year long no matter where you live in the world.

Let's listen to some of the different types of tropical plants that you can grow in a greenhouse. Typically, people grow plants in the greenhouse has to provide food for themselves or to sell the food that they grow. So, why would you want to have a greenhouse filled with plants that you cannot eat? One answer to this is that tropical plants are relaxing and refreshing. When you are able to walk out and surround yourself in a humid, warm environment that is filled with green and beautiful leaves, you may find yourself with less stress and in an overall happier mood. It is also fun to grow tropical plants in greenhouses because they are beautiful. There's something that people want to be able to enjoy all over the world but they cannot when the climate is too cold for them.

Typically, if you want to have a tropical greenhouse, you might want to have a large space. This is because a lot of the beautiful tropical plants are fairly large. If you have a larger space, you will be able to fit these big plants—if you could even grow a tropical plant that grows food that is large, like a banana tree. Banana trees are fun because they produce large amounts of bananas all the same time and because they are beautiful to look at. Even when they do not have food on them, and they are a majestic plant.

There are many types of tropical plants. You can grow fruit trees, flowering plants, or things like palm trees. You can grow all sorts of things depending on what you want to look at or what you want to benefit from. You can design your tropical greenhouse to have plants that remind you of a certain area of the world or do you have plants that are useful to you in ways of giving you food or in ways of helping you with medicine like that aloe vera plant. There are many different ways that you can use tropical plants. Even if they do not seem to have a use, they may just help you to feel happy, and they may make a great space for you to spend time in.

When you have a tropical greenhouse, you will have to pay special attention to the lighting and heating. Tropical greenhouses obviously need more light and more heat. They need to be extra humid, so you may want to have a missing or dripping system to allow this to work.

Even though tropical greenhouses may require a lot of work for a lot of extra equipment, they are still a good choice if you love the warm areas of the world. You can create this face right in your backyard. They are fun, and they're useful. They have many benefits. If you would like to grow a tropical greenhouse, we encourage you to give it a try. We do not think that you will be disappointed.

A different type of greenhouse growing that we are going to look into is called hydroponics. It is not necessarily a type of thing that you can plant in your greenhouse, but it is a way of planting. It is a way of planting that when many people start, they stick with it. Typically, people either plant normally or they plant hydroponically. Let's look into what hydroponics is.

Hydroponics is a way of growing plants without dirt or soil. Typically, hydroponics is grown in water or material like perlite. This unique writing system gives many benefits to the plants that are grown in this way. It allows the ribs of the plants to soak water in well and it allows the roots of the plants to gain all of the nutrients that are available for them as well.

A lot of people who use hydroponics are big-time gardeners. Because of this, they may also have greenhouses as well. If you would like to use hydroponics in your friend's house, it is definitely something that you can work out. To use hydroponics near the greenhouse, you simply need to set hydroponic systems up instead of using dirt and containers. It is just like having a normal greenhouse, but you use your hydroponic system instead.

Through hydroponics, you can grow any type of plant. You can grow fruits or vegetables just like we were talking about earlier. The only difference is how you would plant them. They would still give you the same benefits if you planted them hydroponically.

One downside of planting your plants in your greenhouse through the hydroponic way is that it can be expensive. You need to buy a lot of material that is not as cheap as small plastic containers that hold dirt. If you do like hydroponics and you are willing to spend the money on it, however, it can still be a good choice.

Hydroponic greenhouses can look just like normal ones. They can still be designed to maximize space and can still be grown vertically in many circumstances. They can still girl any of the plants that can be grown in soil. They still need greenhouse essentials, and they still need to be prepped for every season. Basically, hydroponic greenhouses are just like normal greenhouses except for the growing media that is used to put the plants in. No matter how you choose to plant your plants in your greenhouse, almost everything you do will be the same. You will still get great results from your structure either way.

It is clear that there are many different things that you can plant in greenhouses. Greenhouses are made for just about any type of planting. There are no restrictions on what you can grow inside of them. All you need to ensure is that what you are growing fits inside of the greenhouse and that you are able to provide the plants with what they need in terms of heat, humidity, watering, etc. When you are choosing what to grow in your greenhouse, consider that you could grow fruits, vegetables, herbs, tropical plants, or you could grow these things through hydroponics. Also, consider that you could choose a mix of all of these things. Look into these ideas in detail, and decide which ones excite you. Figure out which ones will benefit your life the most. When you have found some answers to what you would like to plant, go ahead and start the process. We know that no matter what you choose, your greenhouse will be full of things that you enjoy and things that will benefit your life greatly.

CHAPTER EIGHT
Starting Seeds

One of the best ways to get the plants to grow in your greenhouses by planting seeds. Seeds are available to buy at a very low price point when compared to buying entire plants. They are also rewarding. When you decide to plant a seed, and then it sprouts, you get the satisfaction of helping that tiny seed to turn into something great. Seeds are a great thing to plant inside of your greenhouse. In this chapter, we will look into how to start seeds in your greenhouse.

There are two different reasons why you would want to plant seeds in your greenhouse. The first of these reasons is that you are wanting to get a head start on growing plants that can be transplanted into your outdoor garden once the weather is nice enough.

If you want to start seeds to transplant into your outdoor garden, you will want to start them in your greenhouse so that they are able to grow when the weather is still too cold for them to grow outside. Typically, you are going to want to plant your seeds about six weeks before the last estimated frost date in your area. You cannot put your seeds outside before the last frost date as we mentioned earlier. However, if you start your seeds in the greenhouse, your plants will be mature and ready to go by the time that the last frost happens. This will make your harvest be able to happen earlier, and it will increase the odds of your plants surviving outside since they already got a good strong start in your perfect greenhouse environment.

The other way that you can start seeds in a greenhouse is if you want them to live in your greenhouse for their entire life span. In this method, you would start your seeds in your greenhouse in you would keep the plants in your greenhouse all the way through harvest time. If you choose this method, you can choose to plant your seeds that any time of year that you would like to.

Let's look into how you can grow seeds in your greenhouse. The most commonly used way of planting seeds in a greenhouse is through the soil. You will need a few different things for this process. You will need two containers, soil, and seeds. Each type of seed is different—but typically, all you will need to do is fill your container with soil, make a small hole for the seed, and cover it up. You will then need to water the seed often until it sprouts. Once it sprouts, you will need to continue to care for it by watering it often and making sure it has adequate light and fresh air. Growing seeds in a greenhouse is a fairly simple process, and it is basically just the same as if you were growing them inside of your house or in a garden.

You can also grow seeds in a greenhouse through hydroponics. If you choose this method, you will be planting your seeds in water or a different growing media like perlite. You will still need to make sure that your plant has what it needs before and after it sprouts.

There are a few different tools that can make growing seeds in a greenhouse much easier. The worst thing that can make growing seeds in a greenhouse easy is the type of tray that you choose to use. You can choose to use a tray that has individual pockets for each seed to grow in. These trays are nice because you know that you planted one seed in each pocket.

You can also grow your seeds in a plain, flat tray. If you choose to do this, you will just want to poke holes into the soil where you want your seeds to grow. You will not have specific pockets for each need to go in, so you can just pick a spot. You will want to make sure that your seeds are spaced appropriately from each other so that they have space to grow. Typically, this is the spacing that is close to 1 or 2 in part for each seed. However, the exact spacing that you need to follow will usually be listed on the back of the package of seeds. It depends on the type of seed in many circumstances.

Now that we have looked at the basics, let's talk through some tips and tricks that can help you to grow the best plants from seeds. This is one way to grow seeds. There are other ways that you can do so successfully, but we believe that this method is strong and that it works well. Because of this, we are going to explain this method and details so that you are able to use it in your own greenhouse seed sowing if you want to.

You will need to get your trays ready. We recommend the trays that have a pocket for each seed. This is because they are the easiest to use. They help each plant to stay separate, and they helped to make sure that you are giving each seed enough space to grow. The trays that have separate containers for each plant have more benefits as well. For example, these trays are better at providing warmth and moisture to each separate seat. This is because the moisture and warmth stay in a certain area to protect the seed and it does not spread out through the entire container. It is also better because it keeps the roots of each plant in their own space. If you use a tray that is flat and has many seeds in the same opening, their roots often become entwined with each other. When the roots of the plant become entwined with those of the plants around it, it hurts their survival rate greatly. This is because, in order to separate the plants, like you will have to do to move them into larger and deeper containers, you have to separate the roots. If you break the roots of the plant, it is much harder for the plant to survive. The roots are a very important part of the plant, and you do not want to break them or hurt them in any way.

After you get your trays, you will want to fill them with soil. We recommend starting with a seed starting mix. This is because seed-starting mixes have all of the nutrients that you will need in order to start your seeds successfully. If you use a different type of potting mix, your seeds may still come up, but the success rate is lower than if you choose a potting mix that is specifically made for seeds and nothing else.

You can buy the seed starting mix at a store, or if you feel like making your own, you can use that option as well. If you want to make your own seed starting mix, you can start with a typical potting mix that you would find at any store. You would then want to add a few things to it. You would want to add equal parts of perlite, peat moss, and organic compost. Adding these things to your regular soil will make the soil have just the right nutrients that your seedlings need to have a strong beginning of life.

Making your own soil can be a good option, especially if you are on a budget or if you simply like to make things yourself. However, it is important to know that it is best to use new soil when you are planting seedlings. If you do happen to reuse soil that you have used in seedlings or in other plans in the past, you need to sterilize this soil. This is because some germs or diseases that plants can get could be in that soil. If you plant your seedlings into the soil, they either will not sprout, or they will grow diseased plants. This is not what you want, of course. You want healthy seeds so you will need to start with healthy soil.

Once you fill your tray with soil, it will be time to plant your seeds. You will want to push your finger into each seed pocket filled with soil to make a small indentation. Inside this hole, you will want to place two to three seeds. It made me feel silly to put 2 to 3 seeds inside each pocket when you only want one plant to grow. However, we believe that this is the best option. This is because not every seed is going to be successful and its mission to turn into a sea link. If you plant two to three seeds inside of each pocket, you have a much better chance that at least one of them will have enough luck in surviving. If you do happen to have two or even all three of the seeds make it and turn into seedlings, you will need to trim the seedlings that are the least strong. For example, if you have three seedlings come up in one container and one of them is tall, one of them is short, and one of them is tipping over—you will want to trim the one that is short in the one that is tipping over. This leaves the strongest and tallest seedling in your tray so that you are able to grow it into a mature plant. The strongest and tallest seedling is chosen because it has the best chance of surviving all the way through until it grows a crop and is able to be harvested from.

It is important to note that some seeds need extra care before they are planted. Larger seeds from plants like peas, pumpkins, and squash need to be soaked before they can be planted. This helps them to sprout easier and faster since they have such a hard shell. You do not want to soak all seeds, however, because small seeds like those of tomatoes and carrots can be really hard to handle after they are soaked and they don't need to be soaked anyway. Because of this, you will want to research what each type of seed needs before you decide to plant it.

After you plant your seeds, you will want to cover them with the soil. You can either use extra soil for this or simply push the soil over that you use to make the hole earlier in the process. Either way will work just as well, so this decision is just up to your own judgment and what you feel will be easiest for you.

Once your seeds are planted and covered up with soil, it is time to care for them. In regards to the temperature of your greenhouse, most seeds germinate best if they are kept at a temperature that is between 70 and 80 degrees Fahrenheit. At night, this temperature can dip down to between 50 and 60 degrees Fahrenheit. You will want to keep your greenhouse at this temperature with either the use of sunlight or the use of heaters. If you do not have these temperatures in your greenhouse, your seeds may not do as well as you are hoping that they will do. If you have a greenhouse that is not warm enough but can still grow seedlings, you can consider something called a seedling heat mat. These are heat mats that go on the benches in your greenhouse. You can then put your trays filled with seedlings on top of them. These heat mats help the soil to stay the right temperature for the seeds. Even if the air is the wrong temperature, if the soil is the right temperature, your seedlings can have a successful start to their life.

Another trick that you can try with growing seeds is to cover your plants up before they sprout. Sometimes, seeds do best when they are covered during their germination. Once they sprout, though, you need to uncover them right away—this is because that is the time when they will start to need light to grow healthily.

Tips for growing seeds in a greenhouse is to record the results of your crops. If you grow a batch of seedlings one day after soaking your seeds in water, write down what you did to them before planting them and then write down how they end up sprouting. Compare your results to a crop that you did not soak in water. Using this technique, you will be able to tell if you are tips and tricks that you are using for your seed starting are working or if they are not working at all. Using this technique, you will also be able to tell what works best for you and what really doesn't work. Once you have planted many batches of seeds and tried out many different tricks, you will be able to find the very best way for you to grow seedlings in your greenhouse.

Overall, growing seedlings in your greenhouse is a great thing to do. Starting plants from seeds not only saves money, but it is also a very rewarding process. You'll get to take something so small, and turn it into something large. You can take one tiny seed and turn it into a plant that can feed you multiple times throughout the year. When you are growing seeds, remember to start them in either a flat open tray or a tray that has multiple openings for the seeds. Remember to put money seeds in each hole so that at least one comes out, and then pick the strongest seedling to be the one that survives. Remember to use an appropriate soil mixture for seed starting whether that means making your own seed starting mix or buying a seed-starting potting mix from the store. Remember to keep the temperature of your greenhouse correct and make sure that your plants are getting adequate water and light. Water your plants off so that they are able to grow strong. Try out different growing techniques if you want to see if you can get your plants to grow faster than normal. Try covering your soil during the germination. Or try soaking your seeds in water before you plant them. Remember to write down your results so that you are able to compare what works and what doesn't work for you specifically in your greenhouse. Growing seeds in your greenhouse is a great adventure, and we know that with the tips and tricks in this chapter, you will be able to have great success.

CHAPTER NINE
Caring for Your Plants

Whether you choose to start your plants from seeds or buy plants from the store, the next step in the process of growing in your greenhouse will be to take care of your plants. This may be the step that you have envisioned yourself doing the most so far. You may have been picturing yourself walking out into your greenhouse to be surrounded by life. You may have seen yourself watering plant after plant—maybe even letting a little bit of the cool water touch your toes in the hot and humid greenhouse air. You may have been looking forward to creating the perfect feel for your favorite plants or harvesting your favorite fruits and vegetables. In this chapter, we are finally going to talk about all of these fun topics. In this chapter, we are going to discuss temperature, lighting, watering, pollination, and harvesting crops in detail.

First, let's begin to discuss temperature. Temperature is the biggest reason why greenhouses are such a useful tool in gardening. When you are using your greenhouse, you can control the temperature in three different ways. We will look into each of these two ways in detail below.

The first way that you can control the temperature of your greenhouse is through the use of the sun. The sun is the natural heating source that greenhouses really on for a majority of their heating needs. One of the first ways that you can ensure that you are able to use the sun as a heating source is by placing your greenhouse in a good location. Preferably, you want to place your greenhouse on the south side of your property. As we mentioned a little bit earlier, the south side of your home is usually the area on your property that gets the most sun. However, if the south side of your property has the sun blocked by other houses or is lined with tall, sun-blocking trees, you would want to choose a different part of your property and likely a different side of your home. The most important thing to do when choosing a location for your greenhouse with temperature in mind is to make sure that you are choosing the sunniest location possible.

It is true that greenhouses can get too hot. However, a hot greenhouse is much easier to cool down than a cold greenhouse is to warm up. Because of this, the sunniest location on your property is almost always the best choice for the location of your greenhouse in regards to temperature. If the sun does make your greenhouse too hot, you still have options to help you give your plants the environment that is absolutely perfect for them. You can use sun shades, which we also talked about a little bit earlier. Sun shades are a great temperature control product. They can be spread across the roof of your greenhouse if you are getting too much heat from the sun. They can cover your entire roof or just a portion of it. They can be used for any time span that you need to use them for. With this much versatility, sun shades are the perfect tool to use if you need to naturally bring the temperature of your greenhouse down due to it having too much sunlight.

Sometimes, however, sunshades may not be enough. This point brings us to our second tool that can be used to control the temperature of a greenhouse. If the sun shades are not enough, you may need to rely on air flow to help you cool the temperature of your greenhouse. You can gain air flow by the use of vents or opening windows if the air outside has a cool breeze. If your greenhouse is too hot and the outside air is too hot and humid as well, however, you will need to rely on fans for your air circulation instead. As we mentioned earlier in the book, almost all greenhouses need fans for air circulation anyway. This makes this temperature cooling technique easy and accessible to almost all greenhouse gardeners.

Next, let's look into our third and last temperature controlling technique. Sometimes your greenhouse will not be too hot. In fact, at times it will probably become much too cold. If the sun is not enough to warm the temperature of your greenhouse, you will need to use heaters. Heaters are a strong tool that you can use to create the perfect air temperature that your plants need. Heaters are often needed to control the temperature of your greenhouse during the winter and possibly even during early spring and late fall in the colder areas of the world.

So now that we know ways that you can make your greenhouse warmer or colder, why do you need to do this in order to care for your plants? You need to control the air temperature that surrounds your plants because plants cannot grow in any temperature. They need to have the correct climate feel and growing environment. This means they simply will not thrive and may not even survive if they are not grown at the right temperature. When you are growing your plants, it is important to read up on each specific plant type that you choose to grow. Check what their optimal temperature is or look at what the temperature typically is in the area of the world that they are native to. Then, work to match the temperature of your greenhouse to the number that you find.

It is also important to note when looking at caring for your plants in your greenhouse in regards to temperature, that every plant in your greenhouse does not need to be grown at the same temperature. You can successfully grow plants that need different climate feels inside of the same greenhouse. To do this, you simply need to use artificial lighting.

That brings us to our next way to care for your plants. Let's look into lighting, why your plants need it, and how you can use it inside of your own greenhouse to create the perfect environment for your plants to live in. Of course, the most important and most well-working light that plants need comes from the sun. The sun provides natural light that oftentimes is something that you do not even need to think about. However, sometimes, in greenhouse gardening, your plants will need more light than the sun is able to provide in your area at a specific time of year. Let's look into how you can use artificial light to your plants when these situations arise.

First, let's look into the most common time that greenhouse gardeners find they need to use artificial light. This time is during the majority of the winter season. This is because during winter, the sun is both farther away and it does not shine for as many hours in the day. This makes the plants that are located in greenhouses not get enough sunlight.

Even if plants are kept warm enough through the use of heaters, they still need adequate time in the sunshine. This is because plants need sunlight in order to survive. Sunlight is the power behind photosynthesis. Photosynthesis is the process that plants use to make their food. They take the carbon dioxide that they breathe in and combine it with the water they take in to create their own food. Without the sun shining on them, they would not be able to do photosynthesis in order to make food for themselves, and they would starve. This information shows us that if plants do not get adequate sunlight, they will not survive.

Luckily, artificial light can be the power behind the photosynthesis process as well. If you are growing plants in the greenhouse during the cold and dark winter, you will need to supplement the light that your plants get with artificial lighting. Typically, your plants will need at least six hours of direct light per day. You can pay attention to how many hours of direct sunlight your greenhouse gets during any given day. You will then need to make sure you provide artificial lighting for however many of the six hours that your plants did not receive. For example, if you look out at your greenhouse and learn that it is getting only four hours of direct sunlight per day, you will need to give you plants two hours of time under artificial lighting to keep them healthy.

You also need to look at how much daylight a plant is receiving, even when it is not sitting in direct sunlight. This type of light that a plant needs in a day is called a photoperiod. In the winter, our days are short and our nights are long. During this time, you will want to provide additional lighting to give your plants inside of your greenhouse the feel of longer days. These are called photoperiod control lights. If you want your plants to be successful, you should consider adding these lights to your greenhouse plant care routine as well.

Growing plants with artificial lights and without much sunlight at all can be an option as well. Of course, it is preferable to give your plant as much sunlight as possible. This is because sunlight is natural, it is free, and it is what plants are truly seeking. However, if for some reason you need to grow plants under artificial lights you should know that it can be done. This technique would be helpful if you are using one of the space-saving methods that we talked about earlier in the book. For example, if you are growing another crop underneath your normal growing benches, you will need to provide them completely with artificial lighting. This adds a little bit of extra work to your plant care, but it can be worth it for the added space and the extra crop at harvest time.

When you are caring for the plants in your greenhouse by means of lighting, it is important that you know your types of lighting as well. Fluorescent lights are one option that you can use as a grow light. They do a good job at imitating the sun's light, and they are cool to the touch so they can be placed close to your plants. Another type of lighting that works well in greenhouses is metal halide lighting. This is the best type of lighting to choose if your greenhouse gets no natural light or just a small amount of natural light. High-Pressure Sodium lighting can be used as well. This type of lighting works well in addition to a lot of sunlight and burns hot, so it should be placed far away from plants. Because of that, it is best for greenhouses that sit in sunny locations and that are large in size. The last type of lighting that is commonly used in greenhouses is LED lighting. The LED lighting is very environmentally friendly, and it works well for areas that need their lights to be on for long periods of time and also works well with greenhouses that grow plants in hydroponics.

It is pretty clear that greenhouse lighting is extremely important when looking into the care of plants inside a greenhouse. Remember to ensure that if your plants are not getting enough direct sunlight or daylight, that you are supplementing with artificial light. Remember that artificial light can grow plants without sunlight at all if it is necessary, though sunlight is always the most natural and overall best option. Remember to think about the benefits and downfalls to each of the four main types of greenhouse lighting before you choose one to use in your own space. With these tips, you should be able to grow your plants with the help of artificial lighting with great success.

Watering, of course, is a very important part of caring for your greenhouse plants as well. There are some homemade ways to water in your greenhouse. One of those ways is through an irrigation system, and another is by hand watering. We will look into both of these ways of watering below.

First, let's look into irrigation systems. Irrigation systems can be sprinklers, or they can be drip systems. The sprinklers can be large and on the ceilings, or they can be small and next to the plants. These systems turn on automatically in time intervals that you set them to use. Irrigation systems work best if all of the plants in your greenhouse need the same amount of water. This is because irrigation systems put the same amount of water out in every part of the greenhouse. They might not be a great choice if you have some plants that need to be watered once a week and other plants that need to be watered every day all mixed in with each other. However, you could use an irrigation system even with plants with separate needs if you separated your plants in two different sections according to how much they needed to be watered. It is also important to note that irrigation systems are fairly affordable, so they can be used in many greenhouses even if you do not have a very large budget.

Next, let's look into hand watering. Hand watering can be difficult because it is time-consuming and it can be a lot of work. It definitely takes a lot longer than irrigation systems do because irrigation systems don't require any work. However, hand-watering is free, and it is very customizable. With hand-watering, you will always be able to tell if your plants need water or not. Typically plant should be watered when their top inch or two of soil is dry. Of course, irrigation systems will not be able to tell if your soil is dry or wet. However, if you are hand watering, you will be able to see this, and you will be able to adjust how much water you give to your plants based on how they are looking.

Now that we have looked into both ways of watering and what each way is good for as well as what is difficult about each method, let's look into the watering process, in general. Watering is one of the most important things that you can do for your plants and for their health. Plants need water so that they are able to complete photosynthesis. As we mentioned earlier, plants make their food through the photosynthesis process using carbon dioxide and water. If you do not put water into your plants, they cannot make food for themselves, and they will not survive.

Now that we know how important watering is—let's look into some tips and tricks that you can use while watering. One of the most important things to know while watering your plants is that it is important to water thoroughly. You want the soil of your plants to be watered evenly throughout their service. If they are not, some roots make it too much water, and some roots may not get enough water. If this happens, your plants will not thrive as they should. One trick to make sure that your plans are being watered early is to give your plants a quick rinse, let that water soak in, and then go back to water again. This will help your plants to be watered evenly throughout their entire soil base.

You should also know when watering plants that hand watering can often cause disease to spread among plants. This is because oftentimes when you are hand watering, you may let the hose, wand, or watering can touch the plant and then touch another plant. If you do this and the plan that your test originally had a disease, this disease can spread to the other plants. Because of this, it is really important to make sure that your watering tool is not touching the plants where you water them. A good trick to help with this is to get a watering tool that has a good and spread out water flow. A watering wand or attachment to your hose that allows the water to spread evenly across the plant is a good investment so that you do not have to touch your watering tool to your plants.

Watering is a simple task, but it is something that you need to know about in order to do well. In a greenhouse, watering is an extremely important thing to do. When you are watering your plants, remember to make sure that they are getting the amount of water that they need according to their specific plant type. Make sure that you are watering evenly and thoroughly and that you are not touching your watering tool to the plants. Whether you are using an irrigation system or are hand watering your plants, these tips and tricks should allow you to get the job done well.

Next, in regards to plant care, we are going to look at a topic that you probably never thought of while dreaming about your greenhouse—pollination. In the outdoor world, pollination is done without the help of humans, so it is something that we rarely think about when we think about gardens and growing plants. In the wild, pollination is simply not our job. Even if we create an entire garden on our own, we still leave pollination up to nature. In greenhouses, however, nature is not there to do its job. Because of that, pollination becomes our job and our responsibility.

Before we look into how to pollinate plants in your greenhouse, let's talk about what pollination is exactly and why it is so important. Since it is something that we really never even have to think about, these are the topics that we may need to freshen up on.

Pollination is the process of transferring pollen from one flower to the next. Pollination is necessary to allow a flower of a plant to turn into a fruit. These fruits contain the seeds of the plant so that more plants are able to be grown. Without pollination, plant species would die out. It is their own way of reproducing. It is an extremely important process to the keeping of plants in our world. Pollination is typically done by bees, butterflies, and other types of flying bugs. They fly from flower to flower to collect nectar, and while doing so, they pick up traces of pollen and drop it off onto the next flower they land on. This natural act pollinates the plants of the Earth and allows plants to continue to make seeds and be able to reproduce.

Now that we know what pollination is and why it is so important, let's look into how you can make pollination happen inside of your greenhouse. The simplest way to pollinate your plants inside of your greenhouse is through manual pollination. This is easiest if you have a small garden with a small number of plants, as it can be a time-consuming job. To do manual pollination, you will need to gently shake each flower on your plants to allow their pollens to be released.

You can also use a method called device pollination. This is done with a pollinating tool, which is simply a battery-powered wand that vibrates. An electric toothbrush is able to do the same job. To do this process, you simply touch the device to the pollen in each flower.

Lastly, if you have a large greenhouse or if you do not have time to pollinate your plants by yourself or by hand, you could consider introducing bees into your greenhouse. You can buy bees and let a colony of them live inside of your greenhouse. If you chose this method, your pollination would be taken care of naturally. This is by far the easiest way to pollinate, but before you choose this method make sure that you think through the responsibilities of it. If you introduce bees into your greenhouse, you will not only have plants to keep alive and healthy but bees as well. This can be a big responsibility for some, so only choose it if you are up to the task.

some people may worry about bee stings when choosing to get bees to help with pollination inside of your greenhouse. This should not be a huge concern, however—typically, the bees that are used for pollination are bumblebees, and bumblebees do not often sting at all. Most bumblebees die after they sting, so they use this tactic as a very last resort. If you are kind to bumblebees, they will almost always be kind to you. If you are a family member is allergic to bees, though, this chance may not be worth the risk.

Pollination can seem like a scary thing to deal with in a greenhouse, but this fear is just because it is not something that comes to mind quickly when you think of greenhouse gardening. However, pollination indoors can actually be a fairly simple process. If you choose one of these three pollination methods, we believe that pollination your plants will not be a very hard thing to do.

Lastly, in regards to caring for the plants in your greenhouse, we are going to look forward to one of the most fun topics. Let's talk about harvesting your crop. The whole reason that you plant fruits and vegetables in a greenhouse is that so you will be able to enjoy your crop. The most important part of harvesting is that you know when your plants are ready to be picked. Make sure you know when the things you are growing will be ready. You can read on the back of the seed package how long they take to grow to maturity. You can also research what your produce should look like when it is ready to be picked. For example, you know that your tomato should be picked when they are red and that they should not typically be picked when they are green. This is common sense, but you need to make sure that you are harvesting well in your greenhouse to make sure that you are getting the best crop possible.

Harvesting is one of the most fun parts of owning a greenhouse. With an outdoor garden, harvesting only happens once a year. Luckily, with indoor gardening and greenhouses, harvesting can happen as often as you want it to. In the next chapter, we are going to look into this in detail.

Overall, there is quite a lot of work that you need to do to care for plants in a greenhouse. You need to make sure that they have the right environment and this includes making sure that their temperature is not too warm and not too cold. It includes making sure that they have enough sunlight and enough daylight to provide them with what they need for photosynthesis. It means making sure that they have enough water and that they are being watered well. It also means making sure that your plants have a way of being pollinated, whether that is through bees or through hand pollination or device pollination. If you have looked into all of these subjects and you know how to care for your plants in each of these ways, you will have a very successful greenhouse. When you give plants the things that they need and care for them in the ways that they need to be cared for, they will reward you with a healthy and bountiful crop. Make sure that you enjoy the process of caring for your plants along the way. It can be a lot of work while you are doing it, but being surrounded by life is beneficial for not only the life of the plants but your own life as well.

CHAPTER TEN
Year-Round Growing

As we mentioned briefly in the last chapter, plants in greenhouses do not only need to have one harvest time per year. When you plant your plants in a greenhouse, you can allow them to give you harvest as often as you want to. Obviously, plants will only give you a harvest when they are ready to. However, with the process of growing your plants on a schedule, you can make sure that you have some sort of harvest coming in all year long. In this chapter, we are going to look into how to do this. We will look into how this works and some tips and tricks to help you along the way.

First, let's look into why you would want to have a harvest all year long. If you have plants that can be harvested from all year long, you have fresh fruits and vegetables available to you every day of the year. If you grow enough plants, this could even replace your produce purchases at the grocery store. It will allow your family and yourself to be the healthiest versions of yourself that you can possibly be. It will give you something to look forward to each day, and it will allow you to continue to feel the success of growing in your greenhouse throughout every single season. Having a year-round harvest greenhouse can be a challenging process, and we will look into these struggles below along with the benefits—but it can be a great thing as well.

Next, let's look into how you can make this happen. How can you possibly have a greenhouse that has produce available to you every single day of the year? It sounds like something that would be fairly difficult. In reality, it is actually a simple process. It requires a lot of work and a lot of planning, but once you get that plan into action, I can be a simple thing to follow through with.

In order to learn about how you can make this happen, let us look into what we already know. We already know that you can plant in greenhouses all year long. We already know that you can keep your plants alive in your greenhouse all year long and that you do not need to keep planting new plants for each season. Your plants can stay alive. We know that this is possible through the use of heaters and adequate lighting through artificial sources when it is winter, and we know that this is possible through fans and vents when it's hot in the summer. When you have a greenhouse that is able to be used every season of the year, you can, of course, plant in every season of the year.

No, let's look into what we do not yet know. We do not yet know how you can have plants give you a crop all year long. Of course, you are not going to get a tomato plant to keep producing your tomatoes constantly day after day for years straight. Fruits and vegetables have growing seasons. They have seasons were they grow food and seasons were they prepare themselves to do so. You cannot make an apple tree have apples all year long. You cannot make an orange tree grow oranges all year long. The plants need to have their time to prepare themselves oh, they cannot have food on them every single day.

Because of this, there must be another way to allow you to gain a crop from your greenhouse every day of the year. This other way is by planting your plants on the schedule. When you plant a seed, you know when it will become mature by the number of days it provides you on the back of the packet. For example, if a tomato plant takes 120 days to reach maturity, this will be listed on the back of the seed packet. When you know how long it will take in order to produce fruit or vegetables, you will be able to count on that plant to produce a crop for you at that time. Because of this, you will then know if you plant a tomato plant that you will have tomatoes in 120 or so days. The same holds true for every type of plant. When you plant something, you should be able to tell how long it will take that seedling to turn into a plant that bears food.

Now, if you want to have every month of the year filled with these tomatoes, you will need to plan a harvest for each month of the year. In order to do this, you will need to pick out that month that you want the plan to be ready, and count back 120 days or however long it takes tomatoes to reach maturity. Once you count back these 120 days, you will find that the day that you need to plant your seed on. Columbus Day, you will probably want to plant many seeds. If you plant many seeds, you will have a better chance of getting at least some of them to survive. As we mentioned earlier in the book, not all seeds will turn into seedlings. Because of this, you will want to plant many seeds to ensure that you get some plants out of your effort.

After you have planted your seeds, go ahead and find the next date when you would like a new tomato harvest to happen and do the process all over again. If you want your hair was to happen once a month, you can simply plant the seeds on the first day of every month. Once you have gotten the pattern started, the math will always be 30 days later. Because of this, you can simply plant on one day of the month every month.

If you plant one day of the month every month for a year, you should then have a harvest coming in every single day of the year. As long as you care for your plants in a way that allows them to bear fruit and vegetables, will have your plants set up on a staggering schedule to give you a crop.

You can choose to do this year-round growing with one type of plant or with all of your plants. If you only want carrots year round, for example, you could simply just choose to keep planting carrot seeds when you want them to grow. If you want all of your plants to have a harvest every day of the year, you will do this with all of your plants. Obviously, to do this, you might need a bigger greenhouse. If you only have a small greenhouse, you can consider only doing year-round growing with your favorite plants. If you still do not have space, you could consider some of the space-maximizing techniques that we talked about earlier in the book in chapter five.

Another important factor to consider when growing plants all your robes is that your females need to be ready for every season. If you live in a cold area, you will want to make sure that your greenhouse is winterized and ready for the cold winter. To do this, you will want to use the techniques that we looked at in our Seasonal Preparations and Care chapter, in chapter 6 of this book. You will want to make sure that your heater is working and that it is running, as well as that all cracks and holes that could be in your greenhouse are covered and are not letting air in. He will also want to make sure that any big jobs are done before winter comes so that you do not have to open the doors or windows for long amounts of time as this can make the air in the greenhouse become very cold very quickly. If you are growing your round and you live in a place that has very hot summers, you may want to be prepared with things like some shades and vents on your greenhouse for air circulation. For the spring and fall, you need to be prepared as well. The preparation for these seasons varies based on where you live—but for the fall, you should basically be prepared for winter; and for the spring, you should be basically prepared for summer.

Why do you need to have your greenhouse ready for every season? You need to have your greenhouse ready for every season because you are growing in every season. If you have a harvest every day, that means you are growing every day. This means that your plants need to be alive and healthy every day. In order to make this happen, your greenhouse needs to be repaired and in the optimal environment for the health of your plants as well as their success every day of the year. This means that you need to take your seasonal preparation and care very seriously. If you need a refresher on the details of seasonal preparation and care of, look back to chapter 6 in this book. It has a much more detailed approach to this information.

Another thing to consider when you look into year-round growing is that you need to be ready to do a lot of work every single day of the year. When you do year-round growing, you do not have an off-season. You do not have a break in between crops where you do not need to go out into your greenhouse. You do not have a time where you are not doing multiple jobs at once, actually. You are actually growing seedlings, planting seeds, caring for plants, and harvesting all in the same day. This means that you are around growing can take a lot of your time and energy in ways that typical greenhouse gardening cannot. Of course, for this extra effort, it does provide a lot of added benefits with its increased amount of crop and harvest, but it needs to be a level of work that you are ready for if it is something that you want to consider. This extra work also takes up a lot of extra time. If you want to have a year-round growing garden inside of your greenhouse, you need to make sure that you have enough time to do so. Finding the time to prep for each season, plant seeds, care for your plants, and harvest all at the same time can be really challenging. Year-round growing inside of your friend house is a commitment that you really need to be all in for if you want even to consider it.

With extra harvests, year-round growing also comes with extra costs. If you want to grow plants year-round, you will be buying many more seeds. You will also be buying much more soil, and maybe even many more trays if you cannot reuse the old ones. You will be using more water well water in your extra plants, and he will be using more light to provide the heat and lighting that your extra plants need. Make sure that you are able to cover these extra costs if you are ready to have extra harvests year-round growing in your greenhouse.

Another thing that you should know about year-round gardening is it is great for people who want to sell their crops. If you are looking to sell fruits or vegetables, year-round gardening can be a great choice. If you do your own gardening and sell your crops, you will be one of the few farmers or gardeners who are able to sell fruits and vegetables during their offseason. If you can sell fruits and vegetables during their offseason, you will have a huge advantage over your competition. Typically, people really miss fresh fruits and vegetables in the winter time. If you are able to provide them with you is, you will have a lot of business. You will have a lot of happy customers, and the extra work that you put into your year-round gardening will pay off quickly.

Year-round growing can be hard. Because of this, we want to share with you some pieces of advice. Let's look into some tips and tricks that you can use to make year-round growing easier for you. Our first step is that you should start with a plant. Make sure that you know what you want to do. If you do not have a plan in place before you begin, you are around growing can seem really overwhelming. You need to know what types of plants you want to have and when you want to harvest them. You also want to have a plan for where you are going to grow your plants since they take up extra space as well as how you are going to get the extra resources. You may even want to plan out how you are going to have enough time to spend growing all of these plants at once.

Our next tip is that you should make sure you have a large greenhouse for a creative space plan before planning on having a year-round harvest. It is okay if you have a small greenhouse, but if you do have a small greenhouse, you need to be creative with the small space that you have. Look into different shelving units, or even considered growing one set the plants underneath the normal bench with artificial grow lights in order to maximize your space.

Also, if you are planning on participating in year-round growing, consider asking for help. Ask your friends and family to help you with watering once in a while. Ask your neighborhood children to help you with planting seeds. These are things that your family, friends, and neighbors would probably love to help you with if you asked him. The extra help would also give you the ability to care for plants in a way that you may not be able to do on your own.

Along with that last tip, if you offer some of the harvests to your helpers, they may be much more willing to help. Tell your neighbors that they can take some tomatoes whenever they like if they come over and help water them or help you plant some seeds. If you spread the word that you are helpers will get it back in produce that comes from your garden, you will probably have many more volunteers as well as much better luck getting them actually to come and help.

Our biggest tip for year-round growing is to be prepared. Look ahead at the challenges that you might face. Be ready for what you need to do if you have some sort of greenhouse emergency. Make sure that you understand you will be using many more lights and much more water. Understand that you will be spending a lot of time in the greenhouse. Make yourself comfortable with these facts and even happy with them. If you do these things, it will be much easier for you to grow your plants year-round in a greenhouse.

Even though growing plants year-round in a greenhouse is hard, we want you to find success. We believe that if you follow these tips and tricks and learn all the information that we have shared with you, you will be able to have success at year-round gardening. As long as you have the tools, knowledge, and passion necessary to do this large task, you will have great success.

Overall, it is easy to see that year-round growing inside of a greenhouse is a difficult but rewarding task. It is something that takes extra time, extra money, extra resources, extra effort, and extra dedication in order to keep up with. Along with all of these things, however, year-round growing in a greenhouse also provides you with added benefits. It gives you harvests year-round. It allows you to have healthy food to put on your table every day of the year. It allows you to plan for what you want to eat and when you want to have it ready. It is a rewarding and beneficial process in many ways. Year-round growing can be a great thing to do—you just need to make sure that you are up for the challenge before you begin.

CHAPTER ELEVEN
Common Greenhouse Problems

We have tackled so much information together in this book so far. We have now reached our last chapter together. We have already covered everything that you need to know about building a greenhouse, growing plants in your greenhouse, and finding success in doing so. We've talked about all the different ways of planting and all the different tips and tricks that we have for you. Now that we've reached the end, let's look back and talk about some common greenhouse problems that you might face. Problems can pop up in greenhouses no matter how well you treat your plants. Do you not feel bad if any of these problems pop up? Simply look back at this information and figure out how you can solve the issue quickly and effectively. In this chapter, we are going to go over every common greenhouse problem that you might come up against you in your journey of growing a garden inside of a greenhouse. We will look into the problem in detail, who learn why it occurs, and learn how to fix it. Let's get started.

First, let's look into what to do if you get bugs in your greenhouse. Is there something that you would think of dealing with outside? Obviously, you do not want to need to deal with them inside of your greenhouse. The first reason is that you are already in a structure—you should not have to deal with something like bugs. The second reason is if bugs are in your greenhouse, it is not like they're simply going to be like when they are outside. If bugs are in your greenhouse, they probably think that they are there to stay. You will need to do something to get them out of your greenhouse. They are not going to fly away like they were outside.

Let's start by looking into why bugs get into greenhouses. If there is any space that allows bugs to get into your greenhouse—like a crack or hole or even vent or door that was open for a few seconds—bugs can get in. Bugs go inside greenhouses because they know they're filled with plants and because they want to pollinate them. Bugs can also go to clean houses just to simply explore. Other bugs are looking for plants to eat. Obviously, you really do not want these latter bugs in your greenhouse. You definitely do not want your plants getting eaten by anyone except for you.

Next, let's look into some ways that you can prevent bugs from getting into your greenhouse. One of the easiest ways to prevent getting bumped into your greenhouses is to look at the things that you are bringing inside. If you are bringing inside a plant, make sure there are no bugs in it. If you are bringing in new soil, make sure you do the same. Anything that you bring in should be checked to ensure that there are no bugs that could hurt your plants on them.

Another thing that you can do to avoid getting bugs in your greenhouses to make sure that they do not have a way in. Make sure that all cracks and holes are filled. Also, if you have a fence, you could consider putting a screen on them. You can put screens on the windows as well. You can also make sure that when you come in and out of the greenhouse, you do so quickly and you do not leave the door open.

It is also a good idea to not plant anything around the outside of your greenhouse. If you put plants around the outside of your greenhouse, these plants can attract bugs. If you attract bugs next to your greenhouse, they will likely know that there are plants inside and they will likely find a way in. You want to keep all of your outdoor plants far away from the greenhouse to avoid this happening.

Now, let's look into what to do if you already have bugs inside of your greenhouse. In an outdoor garden, you might reach for the pesticides. This is not a great idea inside of a greenhouse not only because they are toxic chemicals but because in such a small space they can be a hazard. One helpful way to catch bugs inside of your greenhouse is to use bug traps like tape. You can hang out tape all around in your greenhouse, and it will not affect your plants. It will, however, catch the bugs that you do not want to be there. You could also consider making sure to get rid of anything that will attract bugs. For example, make sure that there is no standing water available in your greenhouse. If your bugs are not attracted to anything inside of your greenhouse, they may leave. If you are really having a hard time with bugs in your greenhouse, you could always ask a professional exterminator for help.

Something that can be problematic is your greenhouses diseases. There are many different things that can cause diseases in your plants. These diseases can come from mold, bacteria, and viruses. Greenhouse diseases can be some things that are hard to beat. Let's look into some ways that you can prevent these diseases from occurring in your greenhouse.

What is the most important thing that you can do to prevent disease in your greenhouses? It is to sanitize. You want to make sure that you sanitize everything after you use it. You will need to sanitize 2, trays, and even shelves. If you do not sanitize your tools, it increases your risk of spreading disease inside of your greenhouse from plant to plant. This is because if one plant had a disease and you used a shovel to scoop it out and throw it away, and then use the same shovel in another plant, the new plant would probably get the disease as well just from being touched with the same shovel. The spread of disease in plants inside of greenhouses is really similar to the spread of disease in humans. If you stay clean, you will have a much better chance of not spreading diseases.

You allow someone to watch your humidity and make sure that you are greenhouse does not get overly humid. If your greenhouse is too humid, mold and fungus are likely to grow on your soil. If these grow in your soil, your plants will get the disease because of them. Mold and fungus can also spread very quickly and easily. It is something that you really want to avoid having in your greenhouse.

When watering your plants, you will want to make sure that the tool does not touch your plant's insurgencies, and you will also want to make sure that the water does not splash while you are watering. If water splashes from one plant to another, it can spread disease. Because of this, you will want to use a tool for watering that does not allow water to splash. You will want to use the tool that has a light spray that soaks into the soil and does not splash at all.

Another thing that can help prevent disease is to make sure that plants have adequate space between them. If your plants are too close together, they will be touching each other, and this can cause them to spread diseases to each other. If your plans are spaced apart, when one plant becomes diseased, the ones around it will not be touching it and will likely not become diseased along with it. Sometimes, it can be a hassle to spread plants out in your greenhouse because it feels like a wasted space, but it is better to waste space than to allow all of your plants to become sick.

One last thing that you can do to protect your plants from disease is to look at them every day. Walk around your greenhouse and look for signs of disease. Look for things that look out of the ordinary. If you see a plant that does not look healthy, consider taking it out of the greenhouse and quarantining it for a while. This will allow you to tell if the plant is infected with the disease as well as keep it away from other healthy plants to make sure that they do not catch a disease if it has one. With this process, it is helpful to know what plants look like when they are diseased. If the plant has mold or fungus, you will probably be able to tell right away. If it has mold growing in the soil or mushrooms growing in the soil, it means that it has mold or fungus. This is one of the easiest diseases to tell if your plant has. Another sign that your plant has a disease is that it has large, raised brown lumps on its leaves. These lumps typically mean the plant is sick. Plants that seem to be dying even though you are taking great care of them can be diseased as well. Any plant that is showing signs that are not normal should be taken away from your healthy plants just in case a disease is present.

Next, let's look into what to do if a plant is serious. If you see that a plant is diseased, make sure you take it out for greenhouse right away. This will help to make it not infect other pants. Also, you should look at helping it right away—especially if you are able to save your plant when all signs of the disease are gone and bring it back to the greenhouse. If not, at least, you only lost one plant and not your entire greenhouse to a disease.

Diseases in greenhouses are not fun to deal with, but with the tips in this chapter, you should be able to handle them with success. If you take the necessary precautions to make sure that diseases do not enter your plants and take it seriously when a plant is looking unhealthy, you should have good success in keeping this problem away.

We are going to look into what to do if you look at some plants in your greenhouse and see that their leaves are turning yellow.

Yellow leaves are a common occurrence and plants, but they are not a good sign. There's something that you want to deal with and help right away. If you do not help a plant that has yellow leaves, it is very likely that it will die from the cause of the discoloration. There are many different things that can cause yellow leaves in plants, so let's get started in figuring out what they are.

The first thing that can cause yellow leaves in plants is something called moisture stress. Moisture stress is when a plant gets either too little water or too much water. If a plant is not watered often enough, it will have both dry soil and yellow leaves. If a plant is watered too much, it will have wet soil as well as possible mold or fungus growing in it and yellow leaves. It should be pretty easy to tell the difference between these two problems. You will know if you have been watering your plant a lot or if you have forgotten many days in a row. Even if you do not know this information, you will be able to tell by the moisture level in the soil. If your plant has yellow leaves that have too much water or too little water, it is very easy to fix. Simply make sure that you give your plant the accurate amount of water starting at the moment that you notice the yellow leaves. If your plant is under-watered, you can consider giving it a water soak. To do this, you can soak the plant in water in assessing or in a tub for anywhere from a few minutes to a few hours. If your plant is overwatered, consider giving it some period without water. Once it is dry again, however, make sure you water it normally. Do not wait too long to water it again because then it could turn yellow from not being watered enough.

If you find yellow leaves on a plant and you know that you have been giving it the correct amount of water, think about how much light it is getting. If a plant does not get enough light, its leaves can turn yellow. If you have a plant with yellow leaves and you know that it has not gotten enough lately, considering moving it to a location that it will get more sun in. If you do not have a space in your greenhouse available where this plant and get more sun, you will need to give the plant adequate artificial lighting in order to help it survive. This again is an easy fix. If you find a plant with yellow leaves and it needs like, once you give it light its leaves should correct themselves, and it should go back to being a healthy plant.

Another reason why a plant can have yellow leaves is that the temperature for the plant is wrong in the environment that it is in. If your greenhouse is too hot or too cold, the leaves of plants can turn yellow. Most likely, if this is the cause, many plants in your greenhouse will have yellow leaves and not just one. This is because all of the plants are experiencing the same temperature, not just one. That is one good way to tell if yellow leaves are caused by temperature. If a plant in your greenhouse is too hot or too cold, you simply need to fix the temperature in the greenhouse to allow it to go back to normal. Once the plant reaches the temperature that it wants to have, it should fix itself, and its leaves should start growing green instead of yellow. This again is an easy fix if you notice it while the plant is still able to be healthy.

If you believe that the environment for your plant is completely perfect and that you have been wondering it well, the yellow leaves may be caused by something else. The last cause for yellow leaves that we will look into is plant nutrition. If you have been treating your plant perfectly and it still has yellow leaves, this could be the cost. Typically, you will be able to tell when plants are turning yellow from a nutrition problem because the yellow will appear in strange patterns. It will not just be a yellow leaf for half of the yellow leaf. The yellow may come in lines, or it may appear only in the veins of the plant. Usually, when a plant has a nutrition problem, it is either caused by having too much fertilizer in the soil or by the plant having a disease. If you have been treating your plant and have not put too much fertilizer in it, consider separating the plant from the others to make sure that you are not allowing it to spread disease.

Overall, there are a lot of causes that can cause a plant to have yellow leaves. Luckily, most of them are very solvable and very easy to figure out. If you have a plant with yellow leaves, look back to the chapter or think of the information in this book. When you look at your plants and consider what it means and what it is not getting, you will be able to figure out why it is yellow, and you will be able to fix it quickly.

The last issue that we are going to look at is the occurrence of dying plants. Dying plants are typically caused by one of the greenhouse problems that we have already mentioned. They are typically caused by greenhouse problems that go on seeing, however. Because of this, if you keep a good eye on your plans and watch their symptoms, you should not have to deal with dying plants.

If you have plants that have bugs in them, for example, you should be able to notice the bugs right away. Every time you go into the greenhouse, you should see bugs flying around, or you should see bugs crawling on your plants when you inspect them closely. You may even notice that your plants are being eaten by these bugs. These signs are hard to miss. However, if you miss them, you will start to see dying plants in your greenhouse.

The same is true with diseases. If you have these plants in your greenhouse and you do not notice them, you will eventually have dying plants instead. If you do not catch the disease in time, the disease will spread. They will kill the plans that they have already gotten too, and they will spread to even more plants. If you do not notice diseases in time, they could wipe out your entire greenhouse. This would be a tragedy. It would take all of your work and bring it to a loss. If you do not notice diseases in your greenhouse, you will eventually have dying plants in your greenhouse instead.

Once again, the same holds true the yellow leaves. Yellow leaves usually have easy fixes as we read about just now. However, if you do not notice yellow leaves and you let the plants continue to suffer and not get what they need to survive, you will eventually have dying plants instead. You need to notice your yellow leaves when they are only on a few leaves of the plant. If you notice that your plant is covered in completely yellow leaves, it is probably too late to save.

To combat dying plants, consider simply keeping a closer eye on your place. Make sure that you go out to them and look at them often. Do not solely rely on automatic lights and irrigation systems. Make sure that you were going out into your garden inside of your greenhouse and looking at your plants with your own eyes. Automatic things to help us in our growing techniques are awesome, but they do not replace our human green thumb. You need to be close with your plants to make sure that they can survive.

If you start to have many dying plants in your greenhouse, make sure that you are spending enough time outside with them. Then, look at the common problems that we have already talked about such as bugs, diseases, and yellow leaves, and look at your plants with these in mind. Try to figure out if any of these issues are taking over your greenhouse. If they are, you will know exactly how to solve your dying plant problem. Most likely, the problem will be easy to solve. You just need to see what it is in order to bring it to an end.

Overall, we can see that there are a lot of problems that can go around your greenhouses. Luckily, common greenhouse problems are easy to solve. If you follow the information that you have learned in this chapter and if you spend enough time in your greenhouse with your plants, you should never have a problem with losing a lot of plants. You should be able to see a problem right away and know how to fix it using the right, appropriate, and efficient methods. We know that this information will help you and that you will be able to have success every time you come upon a problem if you use these tips and tricks.

CONCLUSION

We have discovered so much information so far, and we have finally come to the end of our time together. Just imagine—you started this book barely knowing how to garden in a greenhouse. Now, you know how to grow your own plants in a greenhouse that you have built all by yourself. We have covered all sorts of information—from building your own greenhouse and why greenhouses are so great, to the essential things that you need in a greenhouse and to be able to prepare your greenhouse for each separate season. We have looked into what you can plant in your greenhouse, how to start a few things from seeds, and how to care for your plants. We have learned about how to have year-round harvests, as well as how to handle problems that may occur in your greenhouse.

Now that you have learned about everything that you need to know before starting your own greenhouse journey, it is time for you to begin. It is time for you to choose what type of greenhouse you would like to build and where you would like to put it. It is time for you to choose what types of accessories you will put inside of your greenhouse, as well as how you will arrange your greenhouse to maximize whatever space you have available. It is time for you to consider what you would like to grow and what tools and techniques you will use to do so. It is time for you to choose seeds and plant them in soil. It is time for you to care for those seeds and watch them grow and then mature into plants that will give you a crop to harvest. It is time for you to harvest that crop and enjoy it with your family and friends. It is time for you to decide if you want a once-a-year problem or a year-long harvest. It is time that you see struggles in your greenhouse and for you to know how to face them.

Now that the time has come for you to go off on your own, we are so thankful that we were able to help you get to the point where you can be successful in your own greenhouse gardening journey. We know that with the information that you have learned so far in this book, you will grow healthy plants, and you will gain a large harvest.

We thank you for walking alongside us through all of this information and trusting us to teach you about greenhouse gardening. We hope that you enjoyed our book, and we know that you will benefit from the information that you have read. If you agree that our book was helpful, please rate with five stars on Amazon. We appreciate this act greatly, and we will be looking forward to hearing your feedback.

Again, thank you for joining us on this journey, and we wish you luck as you go off on your own!

DESCRIPTION

Are you a lover of plants? Are you looking for a new way to garden? Do you live in a cold climate and wish that you could pursue this passion all year long, even in the winter? If you answered yes to any of these questions, you have come to the right place!

In this book, you are going to learn all about greenhouse gardening. You will start by learning about what greenhouses are and why they are so beneficial. You will learn why they are beneficial to the environment, as well as to yourself and your own life. Once you know a little more about greenhouses, you will learn how to build your own greenhouse. You will learn all about the different structures and types of greenhouses, as well as what each type works well for. You will learn about the best locations for your greenhouse and the different techniques that are used for building them.

Once you have learned how to build your own greenhouse, you will learn all about the insides of these amazing structures. You will learn about the essentials that can help you with daily greenhouse routines. You will learn about how to arrange your greenhouse and how to maximize whatever space you have.

You will then learn about how to plant in your greenhouse. You will start by learning about how to plant seeds and how to actually get them to sprout. You will learn how to care for the plants once they have sprouted, as well as how to harvest them once that time comes. You will even learn some tips for year-round harvesting, which is a challenging but rewarding task.

You will learn about watering plants, keeping your greenhouse at the right temperature, and making sure your plans have adequate lighting. You will get to look into different problems that can go wrong and greenhouses including bugs, diseases, yellow leaves, and dying plants. You will even learn about pollination and how it can be done without bugs.

This book will not only teach you about how to care for the plants in your greenhouse, but it will also teach you about how plants live and why you need to perform each task. It will help you to build a passion for gardening and in anticipation to do each of these tasks on your own.

If you are looking to become a gardening expert in the greenhouse area, this book is perfect for you. It will teach you how to have a garden in a cold climate. It will show you how greenhouses work and how plants live. It can take you from a beginner in all of these areas to someone who knows everything about gardening and greenhouses combined. If you are ready to take the next step forward in this wonderful hobby, turn the page and walk alongside us on this journey. We are excited to have you, and we want to help you learn all there is to know about this subject!

www.ingramcontent.com/pod-product-compliance
Lightning Source LLC
Chambersburg PA
CBHW071508070526
44578CB00001B/480